Supporting Parents of Teenagers

of related interest

**Listening to Young People in School,
Youth Work and Counselling**
Nick Luxmoore
ISBN 1 85302 909 2

How We Feel
An Insight into the Emotional World of Teenagers
Edited by Jacki Gordon and Gillian Grant
ISBN 1 85302 439 2

Helping Children with Ill or Disabled Parents
A Guide for Parents and Professionals
Julia Segal and John Simkins
ISBN 1 85302 409 0

Child Welfare Policy and Practice
Issues and Lessons Emerging from Current Research
Edited by Dorota Iwaniec and Malcolm Hill
ISBN 1 85302 812 6

Next Steps in Parenting the Child Who Hurts
Tykes and Teens
Caroline Archer, Adoption UK
ISBN 1 85302 802 9

Understanding Drugs
A Handbook for Parents, Teachers and Other Professionals
David Emmett and Graeme Nice
ISBN 1 85302 400 7

Troubles of Children and Adolescents
Edited by Ved Varma
ISBN 1 85302 323 X

Supporting Parents of Teenagers

A Handbook for Professionals

Edited by
John Coleman and Debi Roker

Jessica Kingsley Publishers
London and Philadelphia

First published in the United Kingdom in 2001 by
Jessica Kingsley Publishers Ltd,
116 Pentonville Road, London
N1 9JB, England
and
325 Chestnut Street,
Philadelphia PA 19106, USA.

www.jkp.com

Library of Congress Cataloging in Publication Data
A CIP catalog record for this book is available from the Library of Congress

British Library Cataloguing in Publication Data
A CIP catalogue record for this book is available from the British Library

ISBN 1 85302 944 0

Printed and Bound in Great Britain by
Athenaeum Press, Gateshead, Tyne and Wear

Contents

Chapter 1

Setting the Scene
Parenting and Public Policy
John Coleman and Debi Roker

Introduction

For anyone involved in parenting support the last few years have been momentous ones. It is not an exaggeration to say that, in Britain at least, the professional world of those who are committed to developing parenting support has been transformed. Exciting as this has been, it remains a fact that the great majority of work in the parenting field has concentrated on the parents of young children. For those of us who have been interested in the needs of parents of teenagers it has often seemed as if we were voices crying in the wilderness. We are pleased to acknowledge, however, that this situation has changed in the recent past, and it is for this reason that we believe a book devoted to the support of parents of teenagers is timely and, indeed, necessary. Questions of policy and practice are being asked by an increasing number of people, and we hope to address at least some of these concerns here.

Before we continue this chapter we need to say a word about terminology. Throughout the text we will be using the term 'parenting support' to describe a range of activities, including the provision of information, parent education, prevention strategies, empowerment initiatives and parent training. As Einzig (1999) states: 'Parenting education and support is a generic term for a hugely diverse range of learning opportunities for parents' (p.13). We very much agree with this, and we will include a discussion of some of these activities below. For the moment, however, we simply wish to indicate that we use 'parenting support' as the most appropriate general term to cover the activities described here. We should also say that when we speak of parents we are, of course, including all parents and carers, whether they are foster parents, step-parents, single parents or couples.

In this first chapter we will trace some of the reasons for the increased interest in parenting generally, and in the parents of teenagers in particular. We will look at the specific issues which are pertinent to the provision of support for these parents. We will consider how this group of parents differs from other groups of parents, consider government policy on parenting, and outline some current policy dilemmas. First, though, in order to provide some background to the topics covered in this book, we will look at the changing social context of the parenting of adolescents today.

The social context of parenting

It is necessary to commence with a brief review of the social context of the parenting of young people, since without this firmly in our minds we cannot appreciate the difficulties and dilemmas which face this group of parents, and those who work to support them. Much has altered in the last decade or so for young people, almost all of which impacts on the parenting task. The changing nature of the job market, greater numbers in higher education, more young adults living at home, the possibility that puberty is occurring earlier – all these issues mean that the parenting of teenagers poses new challenges for mothers and fathers (Coleman 2000). In addition, as Jones and Bell (2000) note in their excellent book on this subject, the role of parents of teenagers has become more ambiguous, with less clarity about where responsibility and authority lie.

To take one example, let us look at the changing labour market. Since the middle of the 1980s there have been major alterations which impact directly on young people. During the 1980s we witnessed a huge increase in unemployment, and the group most affected by this was younger workers. In addition the number of young people in the labour market has decreased. In the period 1984–1995 the proportion of those aged 16–24 in the UK labour market has reduced by more than 25 per cent (Coleman and Hendry 1999). However this is not the only change that has had an impact on the young. The composition of the labour market has altered, in that manufacturing industry has taken up a smaller share of the total workforce, while service industries have greatly increased. These shifts have meant that young men have lost traditional sources of employment, while young women have benefited because new labour opportunities have opened up for them. Even young women, however, have had to wait longer to start their employment careers because overall the labour market has shrunk.

For young people and their parents the most far-reaching implication of the changing labour market is that economic dependence is delayed. More and more young people now remain in education during the 16–20 year age period, many of them continuing to live at home, or returning home after college. Thus adult status becomes harder to achieve, and greater burdens are placed on parents who might have expected their children to become independent at a much earlier age than is now possible. Such changes alter the very nature of adolescence, prolonging this period and creating substantial economic, social and psychological challenges to be faced both by younger and older generations.

As far as parents are concerned, major issues for them have to do with their roles, their rights and their responsibilities. All these are thrown into question by the fact that young people remain dependent on the family for longer periods today than in previous decades. In relation to the role of parents, it is hard enough to define the role of a mother or father in respect of a 14-year-old. When it comes to an 18- or 19-year-old still living in the family home, things become even more problematic. Nowhere is the question of parental responsibility more acute than in the financial realm. To what extent should parents be expected to continue to fund their children as they become young adults? Here the role of the state is critical, with successive governments seeking to limit benefit payments to teenagers living at home, and to place the burden firmly on the shoulders of the parents.

In the context of the provision of support for this group of parents, we have commenced this chapter with a glance at one major social change which has altered the lives of young people over the last ten or twenty years. The central point here is that social changes which influence teenagers, such as delayed entry into the labour market, may have just as much of an impact on parents. While we have not looked at all the issues which affect parents of adolescents, we have noted some of the dilemmas, and underlined the difficulties faced by parents in this context. Parents seeking to determine the exact nature of their responsibilities have a hard task when the very definition of adolescence shifts in the course of a decade. It is this which serves as a background to the material to be covered in the present book.

Changing government attitudes

As has been mentioned above, at the beginning of the 1990s parenting was not a topic that was high on the policy agenda. A number of factors, however, contributed to a change in attitude. The year 1994 was designated as the International Year of the Family, and many of the initiatives during the year focused on parents. At the same time Pugh, De'Ath and Smith (1994) published a key text, *Confident Parents: Confident Children*, which made a compelling case for the development of better support systems for all parents, but especially for those belonging to vulnerable groups. Celia Smith (1996) followed this up with a review of parenting programmes in the UK, documenting the growth of group-based parenting support initiatives. At this stage there was still little public interest in the parenting of teenagers, and Smith's review only mentioned a handful of programmes aimed at this group of parents. At the Trust for the Study of Adolescence (TSA) we were convinced that there was a need for a closer look at this particular sector. In our own review (Roker and Coleman 1997) we were able to identify over 60 programmes aimed at parents of teenagers, but we also noted that more resources and evaluation were essential if this area of parenting work was to thrive.

It became clear from the outset, in May 1997, that under a Labour government parenting was to receive much greater support than had been the case previously. A range of new policies was developed, and funding opportunities for parenting work became more widely available. Key factors in the changing climate included the establishment of the Ministerial Group on the Family chaired by the Home Secretary, the publication of the Consultation Document *Supporting Families*, the expansion of the telephone helpline renamed Parentline Plus, and the establishment of the National Family and Parenting Institute. All these sent out a message indicating that parenting support was to be a priority for this government. In addition the Home Secretary established within the Home Office a special unit, the Family Policy Unit, which has had both a grant-giving and policy formulation role. In 2000 a special programme was announced by this unit, specifically directed at developing new initiatives to support parents of teenagers.

A further boost to this area has come from the new criminal justice legislation. An important element of the Crime and Disorder Act (1998) is the section on the responsibilities of parents, and the provision made for the introduction of Parenting Orders. While there have been some objections to the notion of Parenting Orders on civil liberties grounds, there is also accumulating evidence that most parents of young offenders, after some initial hostility, have welcomed the support offered through the scheme. Further discussion on this topic will be found in Chapter 5. For the present we may note that government policy in the youth justice arena has served to focus attention on parenting support, and has undoubtedly acted as a spur to the development of new materials, new training and new programmes.

As will be apparent, a variety of factors have contributed to the change in public attitude regarding parenting support for parents of teenagers. As we shall see below, there remain a number of controversial areas, and some unresolved policy dilemmas facing the government. Nonetheless it has to be acknowledged that there has been a sea change in the way in which this area of work is perceived today, and particular government ministers, especially the current Home Secretary, Jack Straw, have had an important role to play in making this possible.

Parents of teenagers are different

In considering the question of support for parents of teenagers it is fundamental that we recognise the particular characteristics of this group. All too frequently it is assumed by those developing policy in this area that parenting support for parents of teenagers is no different from any other parenting support. This is not the case, and it is essential to be clear about some of the key differences between parents of young children and parents of teenagers.

In the first place, parents of teenagers are more isolated than other parents. They do not gather at the school gates, and they receive less support from other parents mainly because there is no acceptable setting where they can get together. Related to this is the fact that this group of parents is more difficult to access. Because there is no obvious gathering place, there is no simple way to get information to them, or to offer informal opportunities for advice and support.

In the second place, parents of adolescents are likely to be at a different stage of the life course from parents of younger children. They will be older, more likely to face health or employment problems, and more likely to have responsibilities for their own parents as well as their teenagers. Their own relationships with partners may also be under strain, with the optimism and closeness of early marriage giving way to a less satisfying family life. In addition to all this they may find that, just when they expect to be free of the financial burdens of looking after teenagers, their young people continue to live at home, and to expect further financial support.

Finally, the parenting of teenagers does have particular types of challenges, and in many respects is more difficult than the parenting of younger children. Young people are skilled at finding ways to infuriate and distress their parents. Furthermore, parents of teenagers may be likely to feel more shame for what is perceived as parenting failure. This is partly because teenage behaviour is more visible in the community, and perhaps also because when teenagers are in trouble their behaviour may have more long-term consequences.

To emphasise the differences between parents of teenagers and other parents is also to raise the question of the nature of appropriate support for this group. It is clear that we have to think about support in a different way if we are considering a group who do not normally come together, and who may feel guilty and ashamed of the behaviour of their offspring. Support can take many forms, and in the course of this book various authors will be outlining a range of options. For the moment we may note that support can mean the provision of good quality information, it can mean one-to-one advice at the point of need, it can mean an ongoing support group, or in some cases it can mean family therapy. In the course of the book we will be looking at some of the indications for the use of these various forms of support, and the strengths and weaknesses of each approach. For the present it is sufficient to make the point, for policy makers and practitioners alike, that parents of teenagers have support needs that are clearly different from those of other groups. We will now turn to a consideration of some current policy dilemmas.

Some policy dilemmas
The role of government
In many respects it should be acknowledged that the government has shown considerable courage in tackling this field of work, since it is hardly untouched by dilemmas and difficulties. In the first place there is the question of whether government has a role at all in this type of family policy. In the early days of the Labour government there was much discussion in the media about where the boundary lay between interference and appropriate involvement. There are some who view the family as a private institution and believe that, except in extreme cases, it should be largely free from state interference. On the other hand there are those who take the

position that government does have a role in enhancing support for the family and in modifying attitudes about the importance of parenting.

This dilemma was graphically illustrated by a headline in the *Guardian* newspaper on the occasion of the launch of the National Family and Parenting Institute, entitled: 'Jack Straw plays Spock'. The implication here is that the Home Secretary is attempting to take over the role of perhaps the most celebrated child care expert of the 20th century, and is thereby crossing over into territory which has not normally been the preserve of government ministers. There are a number of confusing issues here. Opponents of the government attempt to portray these moves by Straw and others as being more authoritarian than they really are. If the Home Secretary was telling parents how to deal with a crying baby or a depressed teenager, then he would be a legitimate target for criticism. Of course he is doing nothing of the sort. Rather, he is attempting to create structures which offer more effective support for parents, as well as trying to alter public attitudes to parenting. Perhaps the most powerful argument he and his colleagues make is that at present adults who seek advice and help with parenting are seen as 'failing' parents. The current Labour government wants to reach a position where it is no longer seen as a sign of failure to seek help as a parent, but rather recognised that at times we all need some advice and support in this area of our lives. Many of the government initiatives already mentioned are unlikely to be criticised. No one is going to argue against the extension of Parentline Plus, enabling all parents across the country to have access to a 24-hour helpline, so long as that helpline holds to proper professional standards. Issues to do with telephone helplines are discussed in Chapter 6.

It is perhaps with the introduction of the Parenting Order that the Home Secretary has come closest to crossing the boundary between interference and the respect of privacy. Some of the issues surrounding the introduction of Parenting Orders are reviewed in Chapter 5. For the present, however, we can note that for the law to impose what is seen as a penalty on parents whose teenagers are in trouble, requiring them to receive guidance, is for many people a step too far. Whether in the end parents benefit or not, there is a central question concerning the role of government implicit in the concept of the Parenting Order. It would be unfortunate if it were to provide ammunition which could be used against all the other parenting policy initiatives of the present Labour government.

Parental responsibility

Close to the heart of the debate on Parenting Orders is another key policy dilemma, that to do with the notion of responsibility. Does it make sense to 'punish' parents whose teenagers have broken the law? Where does responsibility lie for the behaviour of a 15-year-old who refuses to pay any attention to what his or her parents say? Many have argued that it is contrary to natural justice to impose sanctions, such as fines, on the parents of a teenager who has become involved in antisocial behaviour. Indeed, some commentators have gone further, arguing that such legal procedures are counterproductive because they bring non-offending individuals into the criminal justice system. This then puts them at risk of further offences (e.g. non-payment of fines, or breaches of court orders) and has the result of 'criminalising' those who would otherwise have had positive attitudes to law and order (Allen 1990).

During the 1990s both Conservative and Labour governments sought to increase the degree of responsibility carried by parents for their children's behaviour. In the Criminal Justice Act (1991) magistrates were given the option to impose fines on parents in respect of offending by their children, and it may be noted that between 1991 and 1998 the number of parents being ordered by the courts to pay fines or compensation has risen steadily (Coleman 1999). In addition parents may now be taken to court as a result of their child's persistent truancy from school, and for other types of antisocial behaviour. While this trend can be seen as an attempt by the state to reverse a perceived increase in youth crime, there is as yet little evidence to show that 'punishing' parents has the desired effect. Most importantly, however, the trend towards making parents more accountable for their children's bad behaviour has distracted us from addressing the more universal question of how long and under what circumstances parents remain responsible for their adolescent sons and daughters. The wider issue of responsibility concerns not only antisocial behaviour but also finance, housing, emotional support and advocacy. So long as parents feel that they are blamed for the negative behaviours of their children, but receive little acknowledgement of their wider role, it is unlikely that we can create a society where growing adolescents get the support they need.

Chronological age

This discussion leads us towards a consideration of another central policy dilemma, that of chronological age and its place in defining rights and responsibilities. The dilemma was well illustrated in the now celebrated Gillick case of the 1980s. Mrs Gillick challenged her local health authority over their right to offer confidential contraceptive advice to her 15-year-old daughter, arguing that to do so would contravene what she believed to be the natural rights of a parent. Mrs Gillick's legal action became a test case in determining how the law should deal with the rights of teenagers under the age of 16, and it went all the way to the House of Lords. Mrs Gillick lost her case, and in giving judgement the Law Lords set out the principal that young people under the age of 16 should be able to take decisions about their lives without their parents being involved, so long as they were 'competent' to understand the consequences of their actions. The concept of 'Gillick competence' has now passed into law, and has had the effect of establishing that chronological age should not necessarily be the determining factor in assessing notions of responsibility.

While this may appear an enlightened approach, unfortunately there remain numerous areas of the law where chronological age is still used as a determining characteristic, as is well described by Jones and Bell (2000). As they point out, age is central to legislation on social security, the national insurance system, the minimum wage, housing and housing benefit, the criminal justice system, and so on. Of course legislation in all these areas is not consistent. In fact the system is rife with ambiguity, to the extent that one set of legislative arrangements can directly contradict another. On reviewing the legislation, as Jones and Bell (2000) have done, one cannot but be struck by our confusion over the definition of adulthood.

While it may be impossible to use the notion of Gillick competence in respect of, for example, social security benefits, there is nonetheless a key dilemma here to do with status ambiguity, and its impact on young people and parents alike. This policy dilemma has to do with notions of dependency. If legislation concerning 17-year-olds gives them adult status in some areas but treats them as dependent children in other areas, the inevitable consequence is uncertainty and confusion. Take housing legislation as an example. Young people over the age of 16 do not have the right to live in their parents' home unless they have permission to do so, while at the same time it seems probable that they do not have the right to hold legal title to land or property until they are 18 (Folkard 1998). Up to this age a tenancy is held in trust for a young person, who becomes a licensee. Other anomalies to do with age and responsibility include the law relating to voting, as well as entitlement to confidential medical treatment. Thus between 16 and 18 an adolescent is truly in a state of limbo, a classic example of status ambiguity.

Conclusion

In this section we have looked at a number of policy dilemmas which have a direct impact on the parenting task. We have considered the role of government in this arena, and we have considered notions of responsibility, dependency and age. If support for parents of teenagers is to be turned into a reality, these dilemmas need to be addressed. A clearer definition of the role of the state, and its purposes in intervening in parenting, would be welcomed. A good but general statement is contained in the document *Supporting Families*, published by the Home Office (1998). It is to be hoped that similar documents in future will address issues to do with the parenting of teenagers more directly. In addition, questions of responsibility and dependency are urgently in need of some clarification. Jones and Bell (2000) have made an excellent start by identifying the issues and highlighting some of the glaring ambiguities in legislation. Further work of this nature would be most welcome.

Routes forward

We shall now turn to a consideration of some conceptual questions which relate to policy, and which are central to work in this field. Most are still the subject of continuing debate, but they are all questions that need to be addressed if we are to take forward the development of support for parents of teenagers. We will consider the differences between support, education, prevention and empowerment, and we will look at the most appropriate points for intervention. We will review the question of universal versus targeted support, look at the problem of how to raise public awareness of the importance of parenting, and finally consider the challenge of finding ways to address the diversity of parenting need.

The definition of support

As we have indicated earlier in the chapter, we have chosen to use the term 'parenting support' as a generic one that covers the range of activities which offer learning opportunities for this group of parents. However we also recognise that, as Einzig (1999) points out, there are key differences between, for example, those engaged in parent training and other types of preventative work, and those offering information and advice to parents on an open access basis, as described in Chapter 9. We discuss this issue further below, in the context of universal versus targeted approaches to parent support. Indeed, these are not the only possible models. Jones (1999) talks of three different discourses in the parenting field, those of empowerment, promotion and prevention. The first, empowerment, refers to a notion of assisting vulnerable parents in being more assertive and obtaining access to resources to which they are entitled. Promotion refers to the idea of making knowledge about parenting widely available. The third, prevention, is closer to a therapeutic framework, and implies that interventions relating to parenting practices can reduce various types of risk. The first two may be considered to fall within the parenting education model, while the last may also be called parent training. Smith makes the point that often these discourses are in opposition, and that, in order for the field of parenting to develop effectively, more thought needs to be given to how they overlap and relate to each other.

Appropriate points for intervention

Turning next to appropriate points for intervention, this has proved a challenge for all those wishing to offer support in the context of parenting. Hinton (1999) makes an excellent point when she refers to family life cycles, and what she calls 'significant transitions' in the parenting life cycle. While it is valuable to identify such transitions, it is still far from clear how these relate to parenting support. If intervention occurs before these transitions or milestones, then this will assist parents in preparing for them. The danger, however, is that mothers and fathers will not yet have had the experience to recognise the significance of the information being imparted. On the other hand, intervention following significant events may well be too late.

Where teenagers are concerned there have seemed at first sight to be two obvious moments in the developmental process where intervention might be appropriate – transfer to secondary school, and the move at 16 to some form of training, or further or higher education. Both these milestones are times when parents and young people have anxieties and questions about the future and seem, therefore, to be sensible moments to plan suitable interventions. The disadvantage of selecting such milestones is that not all young people, or families for that matter, fit a structure of this sort. One girl may have more difficulty in her third year at secondary school than in her first year, while a boy might give up in the year before his GCSEs rather than after he has taken these exams. Nonetheless there seems little doubt that, if we want to choose two useful intervention points during the adolescent period, these are the two when most benefit might be obtained. Planning with schools and local authorities to maximise the impact of any intervention would be a valuable exercise in this context.

Universal versus targeted approaches

A further question in this field has to do with whether it is best to offer universal or targeted support. This is a particularly difficult issue, with important ethical and methodological factors to be considered, and there is a range of arguments both for and against the two approaches. Universal programmes are associated most closely with the parenting education model, as defined by Einzig (1999). These are attractive because they have developed in response to consumer demand and are based on the principle of voluntary involvement. Their disadvantage, however, is that they require large resources to reach relatively small numbers. Targeted interventions, most closely associated with a model of parent training, are more focused, and have the obvious benefit of reaching directly the group defined as being most in need. They avoid spreading the intervention too widely, and thus diluting the impact of the programme. On the debit side, however, targeted interventions for parents of teenagers run the risk of stigmatising the group involved, since they are most commonly directed at parents who, for one reason or another, are in difficulty. Both approaches have costs and benefits, and the choice of a targeted or universal intervention will depend both on the practitioner's philosophy, as well as his or her professional background.

In the final analysis decisions have to be made according to local circumstances, local need, and the opportunities available for parenting interventions. However, it may be that the ideal situation is to have targeted and universal approaches running side by side. Thus, for example, one could imagine a universal service offering support to all who wanted it, perhaps based in a school setting or in the community, with an additional facility for those picked up through the universal service who needed specialised help. A model school-based project which seeks to go some way towards offering just this combination of universal and targeted support is de-scribed in Chapter 9.

Raising public awareness

The raising of public awareness is undoubtedly a major challenge in the field of parenting support. It is a task that was addressed in a symposium or-ganised by TSA at St. George's House, Windsor in 1997 (Coleman and Roker 1998), and has been a central objective of the Labour government as outlined in various policy documents (e.g. *Supporting Families*, 1998). It is agreed by all those engaged in parenting support that greater public aware-ness of the importance of parenting would pay untold dividends in respect of the healthier development of children and young people. However, it is far from clear how to achieve greater public awareness. There are many dif-ficult issues to be addressed if the power of the media is to be harnessed in this way, and without doubt a gigantic co-ordination task will be required at the very least. It is encouraging that the National Family and Parenting Institute is committed to working towards this goal, and in 2000 some ten-tative steps were taken towards the initiation of a media campaign to promote the importance of parenting. It is hoped that there will be more such campaigns in the future.

As one important step, Coleman and Roker (1998) point out that it is necessary to be clear about the objectives of any media campaign. They suggest that a media campaign aimed at raising awareness of the impor-tance of parenting teenagers could spell out that supportive parenting during adolescence plays a part in enhancing school achievement, in reducing offending, in improving self-esteem, and in reducing stress in the home. It might also be noted that improved parenting would have an economic benefit to society. However, no-one should underestimate the re-sources that would be required to bring together powerful sources of influ-ence, such as various media, the supermarkets, the political parties and so on, in order for a campaign of this sort to have a real impact.

Diversity of need

A final issue to be considered in this section has to do with diversity of need. We are used to thinking about diversity in relation to race and sexual orientation. Both these dimensions will obviously have a significant impact on the parenting task, and therefore on the nature of any support that is to be offered. A more detailed discussion relating race and culture to the parenting of teenagers may be found in Chapter 3. Another aspect of diversity, however, has to do with the differing needs of parents of teenagers.

Not all parents want the same type of support. This was apparent in the course of the project outlined in Chapter 9, in which parents were offered a menu of types of support. Some parents might say that they felt lonely and isolated, and that they were desperate to talk to other parents in similar situations. Other parents might say that they would run a mile rather than talk to other parents, but that they would be very happy to have a video to watch at home on their own. Any intervention programme for this group of parents has to take diversity of need into account. It may be said that this is an issue in all parenting work. This is undoubtedly true, but parents of teenagers are a special case. For the reasons set out above, they differ in particular respects from other groups of parents, and cannot be expected to respond in the same way to all types of support. The issue for policy and for practice thus has to do with the necessity of offering a range of options. This may be expensive, but it is critical if the differing needs of parents of teenagers are to be met.

Conclusion

In this chapter we have looked at parenting support in the context of policy developments in the UK over the last decade. We have recognised that there have been substantial changes in attitudes to parenting support, in large measure as a result of the election of a Labour government in 1997. We have considered social changes which impact on the parenting of teenagers, and we have underlined the key differences between parents of young children and parents of an older age group. In the last section of the chapter we reviewed some critical questions of policy and practice which determine the nature of parenting support. This chapter has provided a background which, it is hoped, will inform the material in the rest of the book.

References

Allen, R. (1990) 'Punishing the parents.' *Youth and Policy 31*, 17–20.

Coleman, J. (1999) *Key Data on Adolescence*. Brighton: Trust for the Study of Adolescence.

Coleman, J. (2000) 'Young people in Britain at the beginning of a new century.' *Children and Society 14*, 230–242.

Coleman, J. and Hendry, L. (1999) *The Nature of Adolescence*, 3rd edition. London: Routledge.

Coleman, J. and Roker, D. (1998) 'Parenting and young people.' *The Parenting Forum Newsletter* 10 (Spring).

Einzig, H. (1999) 'Review of the field: current trends, concepts and issues.' In S. Wolfendale and H. Einzig (eds) *Parenting Education and Support.* London: David Fulton.

Folkard, K. (1998) *Housing Strategies for Youth: A Good Practice Guide.* London: CIH/LGA.

Hinton, S. (1999) 'Support for parents at significant times of transition.' In S. Wolfendale and H. Einzig (eds) *Parenting Education and Support.* London: David Fulton.

Jones, G. and Bell, R. (2000) *Balancing Acts: Youth, Parenting and Public Policy.* York: Joseph Rowntree Foundation.

Jones, P. (1999) 'Parenting education and support: issues in multi-agency collaboration.' In S. Wolfendale and H. Einzig (eds) *Parenting Education and Support.* London: David Fulton.

Pugh, G., De'Ath, E. and Smith, C. (1994) *Confident Parents: Confident Children.* London: National Children's Bureau.

Roker, D. and Coleman, J. (1997) '"Parenting teenagers" programmes: a UK perspective.' *Children and Society 12,* 359–372.

Smith, C. (1996) *Developing Parenting Programmes.* London: National Children's Bureau.

Chapter 2

The Needs of Parents and Teenagers

John Coleman

Introduction

In the first chapter of this book we have outlined some policy issues relating to the parenting of teenagers. This provides, we hope, a useful background to the practice issues which are dealt with in the rest of the book. Before we come on to these, however, we believe there is another subject to be addressed which will also provide essential background material when considering support for this group of parents. We refer to the needs of parents and teenagers, and the key developmental processes that occur, in both adults and young people, during the adolescent life stage. We will look first at the needs of teenagers, then we will consider the needs of parents, and finally we will review briefly the lessons to be learnt from research on parenting.

The needs of teenagers

While this may come as a surprise to many adults, teenagers do need their parents. They need their parents for many different reasons – to provide love and affection, to act as advocates at critical moments, to set appropriate boundaries, to offer role models in the development of negotiation and conflict resolution skills, and to provide support in dealing with the count-less daily hassles that we all encounter. All these are important, but perhaps the most critical thing of all that teenagers need from their parents is some awareness and understanding of the process of growing up. Yet because adults and teenagers have very different aims, very different tasks to perform, this understanding is not always easy to achieve. In addition it is remarkable how little most adults know about the adolescent process. One of the most common words parents use to describe their teenagers is 'puzzling', yet they themselves were teenagers once! Many of the apparent contradictions and inconsistencies in adolescent behaviour do make sense, once there is a recognition of the nature of the adolescent situation.

To take some examples, we may note the fact that young people can be fiercely independent at one moment, and childishly immature the next. They can seem to their parents to be nonconformist, while at the same time following teenage fashions and customs like sheep. They may be depressed in the morning, and ready for a party by the afternoon. Similarly they may not want to say a single word when asked about their day at school, and yet by late at night when the parents are ready for bed they may be in the mood for a long heart-to-heart chat. As we have said, none of these behaviours are difficult to understand, so long as it is accepted that the teenager is *both* a child and an adult. The contradictions in behaviour reflect this ambiguous state.

The lengthening period of adolescence

The situation for young people has in fact become even more confused in recent years, as the adolescent stage has lengthened at both ends. It seems probable that puberty is commencing earlier (Hermann-Giddens, Solora and Wasserman 1997), and it is certainly the case that social behaviour in relation to the opposite sex formerly seen in the middle years of adolescence, is now apparent in the last years of primary school. Equally significant is the fact that, as we have noted in the previous chapter, it now takes longer to enter the job market, and it is the norm to remain in the family home until early adulthood. Thus children enter adolescence before they reach their teens, and many are only able to leave adolescence behind them when they reach their twenties. The implication of this is that young people, experiencing a prolonged stage of dependency, become frustrated by being held back and confused by society's mixed messages about adult status. Young people need some recognition from adults that the semi-dependency which lasts for such a long period is difficult to deal with. They also need some action by adults to provide greater clarity about status, and possibly some staging posts along the way so that maturity can be recognised, if not in every area of life, then at least in some areas that have meaning to teenagers.

Negative stereotype

A further important need for young people is to be recognised for the positive contributions they make, rather than face constant reminders of the negative aspects of adolescent behaviour. There is no doubt that there is an overwhelmingly negative stereotype attributed to adolescence in our society today. In films and on television, in books, magazines and newspapers, the world of the teenager is portrayed as one in which bad things happen. Drugs, under-age sex, violence, heavy drinking and many other worrying behaviours are seen as the norm for the teenage population. While all research shows that problem behaviour occurs in only a minority of young people (Coleman and Hendry 1999), the stereotype is pervasive. Research also shows that many adolescents are engaged in pro-social activities, volunteering, campaigning, and helping others in their communities, with very little recognition for this aspect of their lives (see Roker, Player and Coleman 1999).

The negative stereotype has a number of unfortunate consequences. For the great majority of law-abiding and hard-working young people it means all too often that they find themselves treated by adults as if they were trouble-makers. For professionals it can become difficult to distinguish the few who take up so much time and attention from the many who need ongoing support and encouragement. For parents it means that expectations are created about the teenage years which focus predominantly on the problems, helping to fuel anxiety and undermine adult self-confidence.

Summary

In summary, young people need adults around them who are supportive and encouraging. They need adults to have some awareness of the nature of the adolescent transition, and to recognise that the teenage years contain many potential stresses and hurdles. Because the adolescent period is being prolonged both at the beginning and at the end, young people need some clarity about how maturity is defined, and how it can be recognised. Lastly, the positive things that teenagers do should receive more acknowledgement. To be painted as a negative element in society does nobody any good. A greater understanding by adults of the needs of teenagers would do a lot to improve relationships across the generations.

The needs of adults

Parents, too, have needs, although these needs receive significantly less attention than the needs of teenagers. We should emphasise first that it is not just young people who are confused by the question of adult status and notions of dependency. Parents also want to know where they stand, and to be clear about their responsibilities in relation to their teenage children. While there has been little systematic research on the concerns of parents of teenagers (see Coleman 1997; Hinton 1999), we can draw evidence from a range of sources to show that this stage of parenthood is not an easy one. For parents the arrival of puberty brings with it numerous concerns, worries and uncertainties. In the first place the very fact that a son or daughter is moving into a period of life where there are likely to be many difficult decisions to be taken and challenges to be faced is likely to raise the anxiety of any concerned parent. In addition to this, however, there are a number of challenges for parents themselves which make caring for a teenager especially daunting.

Poorly defined parenting role

The first of these is that the parenting role itself is poorly defined. While we all know with a fair degree of clarity what the parent of a 2-year-old should and should not be doing, no such clarity exists for the parent of a 15-year-old. How far is the parent of a teenager expected to monitor and supervise behaviour? To what extent can a parent insist on healthy eating, or the avoidance of drugs, or on tidy bedrooms? At what point do the wishes of a young person override the wishes of a parent? In Chapter 1 we mentioned the Gillick case, which exemplified the clash between the rights of the mother and those of the teenager. If a young woman of 15 wishes to go on the contraceptive pill without her parents knowing, does she have the right to do so? Following the Gillick ruling, the law now says that, under certain circumstances, she does. This outcome has, by and large, been seen as a sensible step forward, and we would agree with this. However, we cannot ignore the further consequence of the Gillick ruling, namely that parents now face even greater uncertainty in respect of their rights and responsibilities.

The nature of authority

The question of rights and responsibilities relates to a wider issue concerning the nature of authority. The authority vested in parents may be expressed through the law and the judicial system but, as we have seen, there are large areas of ambiguity within our legislation. Indeed, a parent might also claim that recent judgements have only served to undermine parental authority, rather than to support it. We live in a society in which the authority of institutions such as the church, the police force, even the teaching profession, is being eroded, and this inevitably has an effect on the authority of parents. It is the generally accepted view that children show less respect for parental authority today than was the case twenty or thirty years ago, and this has profound implications for the way in which adults approach the task of parenting teenagers.

The question of authority is also relevant in the context of the changing structure of the family. As families become more diverse, so birth mothers and fathers have to share their roles and responsibilities with others, or learn to cope alone. The more this happens, the more new questions and dilemmas arise, creating even greater uncertainty for parents of teenagers, a point well made by Walker (1999). The non-nuclear family contains within it multiple sources of stress in relation to parenting issues, and we have a long way to go before these are properly addressed. The role of fathers has been one particular focus in the debate about the changing family. Much attention has been directed towards the difficulties experienced by fathers in creating new roles for themselves following separation or divorce. What is the nature of the authority of the absent father in relation to adolescents, and how does this impact on lone parents and their parenting tasks? Finally, we should not forget step-parents, and the variety of challenges they face in respect of their roles and responsibilities regarding teenage stepchildren.

Summary

To conclude this section, in developing programmes of support for parents of teenagers it is essential that the needs of this group are recognised. We have noted that the very role itself is unclear, and we have pointed out that to some extent this may be linked to the erosion of authority that is vested in the parent. The ambiguous status of the young person has a major impact on the parent, who is frequently as confused about what being 'grown up' means as the teenager. Parents need greater clarity about their role and about their rights and responsibilities. They need some recognition of their own circumstances, and of the pressures upon them. This is especially the case when they are caring both for their children and their parents. Finally, they need more information about the adolescent stage, and greater levels of support in dealing with the challenges they face during this period.

Lessons from research

The confusions and uncertainties identified above lead some people to argue that there are no guidelines as to what constitutes good or effective parenting with this age group. In fact, however, this is not the case, and although there are some grey areas, the research literature provides a range of pointers and suggestions which are available to assist parents. We will now consider some of these, and in particular we will look at parenting styles, the role of parents of teenagers, the issue of control, monitoring and supervision, communication, and the balance of power within the family.

Parenting styles

The first example of helpful research in this area is the work on different parenting styles, first proposed by Baumrind (1971), and further developed by Maccoby and Martin (1983). These authors distinguished between four parenting styles: indulgent, indifferent, authoritarian and authoritative. Those who fall into the fourth group, the authoritative parents, are characterised by the fact that they are warm but firm. They set standards and hold to boundaries, but are more likely to give explanations and to reason with the young person than to be punitive. This classification of parenting styles has generated a large literature, and the studies relevant to adolescents are well summarised in Steinberg (1996) and Coleman and Hendry (1999). In essence young people brought up by parents using an authoritative style do better than others on a range of measures, including self-esteem, coping skills, maturity, and levels of risk-taking.

Steinberg believes that this type of parenting has three core components. In the first place, authoritative parents show warmth, so that young people are loved and nurtured; second, they provide structure, so that the teenager has expectations and rules for his or her behaviour; finally, they give autonomy support, in that they accept and encourage the adolescents' individuality. All these are critical in providing a family environment in which the needs of teenagers are met through appropriate parental behaviour.

The role of parents of teenagers

The next point to consider is the role of parents of teenagers. In a landmark article Small and Eastman (1991) make it clear that research evidence supports a model of parental functions and responsibilities which contains four dimensions. In their view, parents of teenagers should be involved in meeting basic needs, in guiding and supporting development, in protecting adolescents, and in acting as advocates for their sons and daughters. Clearly each function is complex, but Small and Eastman set out compelling evidence to show how, if the functions are interpreted in an appropriate fashion, they contribute to optimal development. For example, under the rubric of guiding and supporting development, they include positive role modelling, setting boundaries, offering examples of conflict resolution, providing warmth and concern, and so on. All these are tied to specific research findings, and overlap with the notion of parenting style outlined above.

Control

As far as control is concerned, this is probably the area in which the largest amount of research has been carried out. Holmbeck, Paikoff and Brooks-Gunn (1995) draw distinctions between power-assertive or coercive control and firm, consistent control. This is a distinction very similar to that contained in the parenting styles concept, with authoritative parenting implying firm consistent control, while both authoritarian and indifferent styles might include coercive control. All the evidence again points to the positive benefits of firm but consistent control, and the negative effects of power-assertiveness on the part of parents of adolescents.

In discussions on parenting style and types of control, one notion often mentioned has to do with the importance of using induction when negotiating with teenagers. Induction refers to the procedure whereby parents and other adults legitimise their authority by providing explanations for the setting of rules and boundaries. Those who use inductive methods also work hard to ensure that young people are able to see things from the adult's perspective as well as their own. This style is associated with positive outcomes during childhood, but becomes even more significant during adolescence. As teenagers grow older they become increasingly unlikely to accept rules and regulations from an adult without explanation, and those adults who continue to expect that this will be the case are likely to experience growing generational conflict.

Monitoring and supervision

The next issue to consider is that of monitoring and supervision. Numerous writers have argued that the more parents monitor their teenagers' activities, the less likely it is that these young people will become involved in high-risk behaviours. Of course there is a fine line between a parent who continually intrudes into the adolescent's privacy by wanting to know everything he or she is doing, and the parent who expresses concern by making sure the young person is safe and properly occupied. The evidence is clear, though, to show that low levels of monitoring and supervision are associated with high levels of antisocial behaviour. In the USA Patterson and others have been active in this area of research (see, for example, Patterson and Stouthamer-Loeber 1984), and in the UK the study by Riley and Shaw (1985) has become something of a classic. However, it needs to be added that recent research (Stattin and Kerr 1999) suggests that, rather than parental monitoring, it is the young person's disclosure or non-disclosure of his or her activities that is the key variable having links with problem behaviour. Stattin and Kerr have shown that parents only know the whereabouts of their teenagers if the teenagers disclose what they are doing. Thus monitoring and supervision is more a function of communication flowing from the young person to the parent, rather than the parent being proactive in seeking information about the adolescent's activities.

Communication

This is a useful point, then, to look at the whole question of communication between adult and young person. Here, too, research provides valuable insights into the needs of young people, and into some of the barriers to effective sharing of information. What is clear is that while both adults and teenagers want more open communication between the generations, numerous obstacles lie in the way of this admirable objective. In the first place there are issues of privacy, with young people needing to stake out a realm that is theirs, one into which parents cannot intrude. Second, embarrassment hinders communication on topics such as sex, while ignorance and possibly anxiety may get in the way of any real discussion on drugs or other risky behaviours.

Noller and Callan (1991) show that the more communication there is between parents and teenagers, the more likely they are to share values and opinions on important subjects such as health, politics and morality. Another key area for research is the power balance between the parties involved in any communication (Coleman, Catan and Dennison 1997). It is often the case that young people perceive themselves to be in a position of powerlessness in relation to adults, and this perception inevitably has a significant effect on the type of communication that can take place. The implication of these findings is that the more parents and other adults can counteract this sense of powerlessness among young people, the more chance there will be of open and effective communication.

Power and powerlessness

Notions of power and powerlessness are not only important for communication, they also have a wider resonance within the family. From very early on parents develop particular patterns of relating to their children, and while there will be enormous variation between families, these patterns are usually based on the assumption that ultimate power lies with the adults in the family. When young people reach their teens these patterns of relating have to be adapted to take into account changing developmental needs. This often means that adults have to surrender some of the power they have assumed to be theirs for a number of years. It goes without saying that this will not always be an easy transition. Parenting strategies which were entirely appropriate for children of six or seven prove to be quite the opposite for those of 13 or 14. Parents have to develop a flexibility and willingness to move to new ways of interacting with their adolescent sons and daughters if serious clashes are to be avoided.

Finally, thoughts about the balance of power in the family lead on to another key concept, that of perceived control. First explored by Bugenthal and colleagues in their work on abused children (Bugenthal *et al.* 1989) and further developed by Goodnow and Collins (1990) in their classic text on parenting, this idea goes to heart of the dilemma faced by many parents of teenagers. Essentially it is argued that the more parents perceive that they are in control, the more effective they will be in managing the child care environment and in providing authoritative rather than coercive discipline. The younger the child, the easier it will be for parents to feel that they are in control. Of course, just because the child is young does not necessarily mean that the parent feels in control, but this can be taken as a general rule.

With adolescence comes an increasing sense of loss of control, although naturally there will again be much individual variation. The notion of perceived control helps us to understand how it feels for parents who believe they have less and less influence over their teenagers. Where parents see themselves as losing control over the young person's behaviour, they are likely to do one of two things. They may become more anxious, and resort to an increasing use of coercive control. It is this group of parents who are most likely to use physical methods of punishment. As we have noted, the outcomes for families where such strategies are used are not good. Alternatively adults who have low perceived control may become depressed, and develop a sense of helplessness about their role as parents. In these situations parents tend to give up, and let their teenagers go their own ways. As we know, this too leads to poor outcomes for young people.

Summary

As we can see, research has a considerable amount to offer to parents of teenagers, and to those running programmes to support such parents. It is not the case that we know nothing about effective parenting with teenagers. We know that the authoritative style of parenting leads to better outcomes than other parenting styles. We know that firm and consistent discipline, clear explanations of rules and boundaries, open communication and a sense of perceived control all contribute to better relationships between the generations. Of course, not all the dilemmas which are faced by this group of parents can be resolved through looking at the research evidence. Nonetheless there is much that is valuable to be gained from the research literature, and it would be a great pity if this was not fully recognised.

Conclusion

One of the underlying assumptions of this book is that the parenting of teenagers is different from the parenting of younger children. This is not only because the adolescent stage has different characteristics, but also because parents of teenagers are themselves in a different emotional and social world, and therefore require different types of support. It seems to us to be essential that those providing support for this group of parents have a clear grasp of their needs. Understanding the nature of the adolescent process, and the impact that it has on those adults who are parents or carers, will therefore be a prerequisite for readers of this book. We cannot hope to cover the whole topic of adolescent development in a short chapter, but it has been our intention to outline some key elements within this area of knowledge, and to emphasise the importance for all practitioners and policy-makers of having a clear perspective on the special characteristics of the adolescent stage of development.

References

Baumrind, D. (1971) 'Current patterns of parental authority.' *Developmental Psychology Monographs 4*, 1–102.

Bugenthal, D. *et al.* (1989) 'Perceived control over care-giving outcomes.' *Developmental Psychology 25*, 532–539.

Coleman, J. (1997) 'The parenting of adolescents in Britain today.' *Children and Society 11*, 45–52.

Coleman, J., Catan, L. and Dennison, C. (1997) 'You're the last person I'd talk to.' In J. Roche and S. Tucker (eds) *Youth in Society*. London: Sage.

Coleman, J. and Hendry, L. (1999) *The Nature of Adolescence*, 3rd edition. London: Routledge.

Goodnow, J. and Collins, A. (1990) *Development According to Parents*. Hillsdale, N.J.: Lawrence Erlbaum.

Hermann-Giddens, M., Slora, E. and Wasserman, R. (1997) 'Secondary sexual characteristics and menses in young girls seen in office practice.' *Paediatrics 99*, 505–512.

Hinton, S. (1999) 'Support for parents at significant times of transition.' In S. Wolfendale and H. Einzig (eds) *Parenting Education and Support*. London: David Fulton.

Holmbeck, G., Paikoff, R. and Brooks-Gunn, J. (1995) 'Parenting adolescents.' In Bornstein, M. (ed) *Handbook of Parenting*: Vol 1. Mahwah, N.J.: Lawrence Erlbaum.

Maccoby, E. and Martin, J. (1983) 'Socialisation in the context of the family: parent–child interaction.' In E. M. Hetherington (ed) *Handbook of Child Psychology*. New York: Wiley.

Noller, P. and Callan, V. (1991) *The Adolescent in the Family*. London: Routledge.

Patterson, G. and Stouthamer-Loeber, M. (1984) 'The correlation of family management practices and delinquency.' *Child Development 55*, 1299–1307.

Riley, D. and Shaw, M. (1985) *Parental Supervision and Juvenile Delinquency*. Home Office Research Study 83. HMSO.

Roker, D., Player, K. and Coleman, J. (1999) 'Exploring adolescent altruism: British young people's involvement in voluntary work and campaigning.' In M. Yates and J. Youniss (eds) *Roots of Civic Identity*. Cambridge: Cambridge University Press.

Small, S. and Eastman, G. (1991) 'Rearing adolescents in contemporary society.' *Family Relations 40*, 455–462.

Stattin, H. and Kerr, M. (1999) 'Parental monitoring: how much do we really know?' *Child Development*. In press.

Steinberg, L. (1996) *Adolescence*, 4th edition. New York: McGraw Hill.

Walker, J. (1999) 'Families and society: change and continuity.' In S. Wolfendale and H. Einzig (eds) *Parenting Education and Support.* London: David Fulton.

Chapter 3

Supporting Black and Minority Ethnic Teenagers and Their Parents

Leandra Box

Introduction

As the introductory chapters have demonstrated, in recent years there has been a huge growth of interest in the area of the parenting of adolescents. This has occurred both professionally, with the development of a number of initiatives on the ground, and publicly, driven by the government's concerns about juvenile crime and antisocial behaviour. Roker and Coleman (1998) reviewed programmes designed for parents of teenagers and identified two trends: first, an explosion of provision in this area; and second, isolated professionals working in a vacuum with limited resources and few opportunities to learn from each other and exchange information.

To an extent, these trends apply to black and minority ethnic young people and their parents. The context of interest in controlling adolescent behaviour applies to these families, while the information in the public domain about the experience of black and minority ethnic families, good practice with such families and materials for professionals to use in working with black families remains limited (Smith 1996; Butt and Box 1998). What has been noticeable is while there has been a growth in programmes designed to work with parents of teenagers, there has a been a low number of black and minority ethnic parents participating in these developments. The problem is therefore exacerbated, for many of those working in this field appear to lack the knowledge and requisite skills to engage black families, and the resources and information on what works is even more thin on the ground and less easily accessible.

Parenting and teenage–parent relationships occur in a context. This context needs to be understood if we are to identify what support is needed and how it should be organised. Some of this context is shared with white communities, but there is also variation in experience between and within communities. There are differences between black and minority ethnic and white communities; and there are similarities of experience between black and minority ethnic parents and teenagers. It is important to distinguish between the issues that most parents and teenagers face during the course of their lives, and those which are specific to black and minority ethnic parents and teenagers (or at any rate different, because of the stresses and strains faced by these communities).

This chapter, then, will explore the issue of providing parenting support to parents of teenagers in black and minority ethnic communities. It will aim to be a resource to those working in the field by: first, providing research evidence and background information on the experience of black and minority ethnic parents and young people in the UK; second, reviewing what we know about parenting in black families; and finally, looking at the support materials that exist, including what kinds of interventions are available and what constitutes good practice in the field.

Black and minority ethnic families in Britain

It is essential, in order to engage and work effectively with black and minority ethnic families, to have a wide ranging knowledge of who the populations are, where they live and in what circumstances.

Of the 3.2 million black and minority ethnic people in Britain, the largest minority community, according to the Labour Force Survey, (Haskey 1996), are 'Indians'(873,000), followed by 'Pakistanis' (543,000) and 'Black–Caribbeans' (509,000). The smallest ethnic group is 'Black–other' (81,000). Although all black and minority ethnic communities are growing, Haskey (1996), in commenting on these estimates and the developing trends, suggests that it is the 'mixed' ethnic group which is growing the fastest. He has estimated that the 'Black–mixed' group may number around 147,000. While black and minority ethnic communities are geographically concentrated in urban areas, it is nevertheless the case that there are very few areas that have no minority families, and so working with black and minority ethnic families is an issue everywhere.

All communities have households where families with children are the single most prominent family type, but black and minority ethnic communities are more likely than their white counterparts to live in families with children. Analysis of the last census shows that:

- of every thousand black Caribbean families, 540 are families with children
- for the Pakistani community, this figure is 810 per thousand families
- for the Bangladeshi community, the figure is 840 out of every thousand.

The comparative figure for white communities is 417 per thousand families. This pattern is true regardless of whether we consider families with dependent children only (children under the age of 16) or all children.

Britain has seen some change in family formation including:

- a decline in the number of families that are formed by married couples (from 83 per cent in 1986 to 71 per cent in 1994 (Haskey 1996))
- a rise in families formed by cohabiting couples (from 5 per cent to 11 per cent in the same period)
- growth in the number of one-parent families.

Marital status shows the greatest contrast in black and minority ethnic communities. Over 66 per cent of Indian, Pakistani and Bangladeshi men over the age of 16 are married, with an even higher proportion of women. In contrast, 47 per cent of men and 50 per cent of women of African Caribbean origin are single (Office for National Statistics (ONS) 1996).

This pattern is reflected in family type too. Analysis of the 1991 census also shows that while lone parenthood is on the increase in all communities, it remains an aspect of how some black and minority ethnic families are organised:

- around 54 per cent of black Caribbean children are brought up in lone-mother households and three per cent in lone-father households
- for children of Indian origin, around 7 per cent are in lone-mother households and around 1 per cent in lone-father households

- for the Pakistani and Bangladeshi communities the figures are 8 per cent in lone-mother and 1 per cent in lone-father households

- for the Chinese community, 11 per cent of children are being brought up in lone-mother and 1 per cent in lone-father households.

As Butt and Box (1998) point out, lone parenthood continues to be seen negatively in terms of family life, and so evidence which shows a higher incidence in certain communities should not be misconstrued. Nevertheless, it is important to note the prevalence of lone parenthood among some black and minority ethnic communities, because of the impact that it has on income and wealth. Despite recent interest in fathers and fatherhood, limited information is available on the experience of black and minority ethnic fathers.

Black and minority ethnic communities and poverty

Research also shows that black and minority ethnic communities as a whole and black and minority ethnic families with children under the age of 16 continue to experience poverty – once again, more so than their white counterparts.

- 82 per cent of Pakistani, 84 per cent of Bangladeshi, 41 per cent of Caribbean, 45 per cent of Indian and 39 per cent of African Asian households have incomes that are below half average income, in comparison to 28 per cent of white households (Berthoud 1997).

- Of lone-parent families, analysis suggests that 70 per cent of African Caribbean, 80 per cent of Indian and African Asian and 78 per cent of Pakistani/Bangladeshi lone-parent households have below half average income (Berthoud 1997).

There is little evidence that allows comparison of black and minority ethnic families' experience of poverty over time (although the findings for the 1990s are similar to those for the little that we know of the 1980s (Amin and Oppenheim 1992)).

Black and minority ethnic communities and education

It is well documented that young people from some black and ethnic minority communities are over-represented in the figures for school exclusions:

- the exclusion rate for white students is around 0.18 per cent, compared to 0.76 per cent for African Caribbean young people

- the figures for African, 'Black–other' and Indian young people are all disproportionately high compared to their white counterparts (Coleman 1999)

- the exclusion rates for Asian communities such as the Pakistani and Bangladeshi communities are also rising, particularly in urban areas

- as are the figures for black girls – although boys remain the predominant group in exclusion figures (83 per cent).

There has been some evidence that racial discrimination may be partly responsible for some of the tensions between white teachers and black and minority ethnic students, with teachers identifying black pupils as disruptive and troublesome and having lower expectations of them (Gillborn and Gipps 1996).

Alongside the evidence on exclusion, Berthoud's analysis of the Labour Force Survey and the Family Resources Survey shows that:

- at all ages until 20, ethnic minority young people have higher staying-on rates than white young people (1999). The same seems to be the case for black and ethnic minority looked-after young people and disabled young people (Butt 2000).

What is clear is that this commitment to education does not seem to result in better qualifications in terms of attainment at 16 years of age: there are marked differences between ethnic groups:

- ethnic communities tend to achieve both the highest and lowest attainment, with Chinese and Indian young people gaining better GCSE results than white students, and African, Bangladeshi, African Caribbean and 'Black–other' students faring worse (Coleman 1999)

- by the age of 21, 64 per cent of white young people in education had gained a degree, compared to 44 per cent of Indians and 28 percent of African Caribbean young people (Berthoud 1999)

- while attainment of qualifications is improving for most groups, this is not the case for Caribbean men in particular, for whom a dramatic decline is occurring.

Black and minority ethnic communities and the labour market

We have already noted that the income of black and minority ethnic families is lower than that of their white counterparts. In addition, changes have taken place in the labour market since the 1970s that have led to greater instability in the job market and increased levels of unemployment. Of course, this has implications for all sections of society, but it has clearly impacted on young people in terms of their expectations and aspirations, and in delaying economic independence:

- between 1984 and 1997 the numbers of young people aged 16–24 in the labour market shrank by almost 40 per cent (Coleman 1999). A proportion of these young people can now be seen in unemployment figures; however, other trends have occurred, such as the growth of government sponsored job training schemes (YTS and the New Deal), and a large increase in the number of young people in higher education;

- traditional sources of employment for men have decreased, while new opportunities for work have opened up for women.

These factors have all impacted on the experience of black and minority ethnic young people, along with an experience of discrimination and institutional racism. The evidence already presented about educational experience and attainment has a clear link to what is experienced in terms of employment:

- young people from all ethnic groups are more likely to be unemployed than white young people: 36 per cent for black Caribbean young people, 31 per cent for Pakistanis and Bangladeshi young people, 26 per cent for Indian young people, compared to 14 per cent for white young people (aged 16–24) (ONS 1998).

Berthoud's study looking at Caribbean young men notes that:

- at the age of 21, 5 per cent of white men are unemployed, compared to 17 per cent of African Caribbean young men
- Caribbean young men who completed their education at 21 are experiencing unemployment rates at almost the same level as white 16-year-olds – despite the additional 5 years invested in education.

In addition:

- when applying for jobs white job applicants are three times more likely to get interviews than those from Asian backgrounds with equivalent qualifications, and five times more likely than African Caribbean people (Commission for Racial Equality (CRE) 1996).
- both Caribbean and African young men earn only 65 per cent of what white young men earn. Even when doing the same job, earnings are lower.

It is also worth noting that where attempts have been made to tackle the high level of unemployment among young people, such as with the introduction of the New Deal by the government, not all groups of young people have benefited equally. Black and minority ethnic young people have not engaged in the programme and gained secure employment out of it in the way that some white young people have (Black Labour Market News 2000).

Black and minority ethnic communities and the criminal justice system
People from black and minority ethnic communities are over-represented throughout the criminal justice system. This clearly impacts on families, but also has a disproportionate effect on the youth:

- black Caribbean people are six times more likely to be stopped and searched by the police than their white counterparts
- in terms of arrests, per 10,000 of the population the relative rates are 117 for black African Caribbean, 44 for Asian and 27 for white people
- this pattern continues, once charged. For example, white offenders are more likely to be cautioned than black, and minority ethnic young prisoners are likely to receive longer sentences than white young people

- the minority ethnic prison population is disproportionately high, making up 18 per cent of the male prison population and 24 per cent of the female prison population (Social Exclusion Unit (SEU) 2000).

In addition, black and minority ethnic people are more likely to be the victims of crime.

Black and minority ethnic communities and racial harassment and abuse

Racial harassment and racial crime are widespread and clearly add to the stresses that black and minority ethnic families experience:

- in 1995 it was estimated that while only 12,200 racial incidents were reported, there were actually 382,000 racist incidents (SEU 2000).

The impact of racial harassment and abuse on families cannot be underestimated, impacting on feelings of safety in the home and community, mental health, and the ability to provide a safe and nurturing environment for child-rearing. In addition the impact on children and young people can be seriously damaging (Childline 1997), and appears to be extremely common in schools, the community, the family, and from institutions (Barter 1999). Discrimination and harassment affect educational achievement and employment, self-esteem, confidence and mental and physical health.

Teenagers and sex

A current government preoccupation is the rate of teenage pregnancy, considered to be worryingly high in Britain, and the highest of all European countries. The focus of this concern led to an SEU report (1999) on this subject that noted:

- rates of teenage pregnancy among black and minority ethnic women appeared to be disproportionately high (although statistics are not collected on a national basis)
- of most concern in this context is the issue of parenting teenagers who have become parents themselves, and parenting teenagers in order to avoid this outcome.

Of equal concern, but less publicised, is the growing rate of sexually transmitted diseases among young black people (Coleman 1999), which has clear health implications and demonstrates a lack or inadequacy of sexual health education, for which the family must be partly responsible.

Adolescence – a time of stress

In addition to the specific problems that black and ethnic minority communities face, which can make the job of parenting and the problems of adolescence even more difficult to negotiate, black parents (like white parents) and black teenagers (like white teenagers) also face a range of common difficulties. These have been well documented and include, for the young person: negotiating the transition from childhood to adulthood; peer pressure and how that relates to drug-taking, sexual activity and criminal behaviour – what we can describe as risk-taking behaviour and independence and how to achieve it.

For parents and carers the issues tend to be around discipline, setting boundaries, dealing with worries about the outside world, including their fears about drug use, crime and violence and sexual health; helping their child to become a socially competent adult, and in addition, adapting to dealing with characteristics associated with adolescence such as mood swings, children guarding their privacy, rebellion, peer conformity and risk-taking behaviour.

Summary

The experience of black and minority ethnic communities must be seen in a context. The context is one where families live at greater risk of poverty, social and economic deprivation, and racial harassment. They most often live in urban areas with the associated problems of drug use, crime and violence. Young people from some of these communities are more likely to be stopped by police and searched, excluded from school, have lower attainment rates (despite higher levels of education commitment), be unemployed, or receive lower incomes. In addition these families battle with racial abuse and discrimination from individuals, communities and institutions.

Negotiating the teenage years is difficult in any case, and parenting through these years is hard, but to do these in the context of the above, as black and minority ethnic young people and parents do, can be extremely stressful. In these circumstances family support services are essential.

Before looking at some of the services that can support black and minority ethnic families, it is worth looking briefly at what we know about family life and parenting in black families.

Black and minority ethnic family life

This area, including parents and their parenting style, has not been much studied (Ahmad 1996), even though it arises often in assessments carried out by social workers of black and minority ethnic families. Shama Ahmed (1986) has provided case examples of how social workers have focused on Asian parenting in attempting to explain the 'culture conflict' experienced by Asian girls. Elaine Arnold (1988) has described the attention paid to physical discipline in work with Afro-Caribbean families. John Small (1982) has described the inability of black and minority ethnic families to be accepted as adopters because of their failure to meet the (white) middle-class standards applied by social workers. More recently research has suggested that this appears to be a continuing issue (Barn 1993; Barn, Sinclair and Ferdinand 1997).

Hylton, in his work with Moyenda on black and minority ethnic parents, draws attention to change in child-rearing practices. Hylton quotes a Pakistani woman:

> Our family system is good but a few years ago English families were like Asian families with similar family values. Now even Asian families have changed for the worst because our children are influenced, they are pressurised in adopting western ways. (Hylton 1997)

Hylton proceeds to draw on comments by a Guyanese man and an African-Caribbean woman expressing similar sentiments. He suggests that these changes in child-rearing practices can be summarised as black and minority ethnic families moving from the discipline of physical control to an emphasis on co-operation. Pointing out that black and minority ethnic parents have viewed these changes as double-edged, he notes:

> Some respondents considered these changes to be a force that has undermined their parental authority, and thereby helped loosen the control they felt they once had over their children. Control of their children is now much more in the hands of state officials such as school teachers and social workers.

He continues:

> In this situation parents believe that the state is destroying parental authority but has been unable to successfully replace it with appropriate sanctions of its own. This has therefore left a vacuum, with the result that some children are out of control.

Dosnajh and Ghuman (1997), while noting change in parenting among 'second generation' Punjabi parents, particularly the greater involvement of men in child care, also record elements of continuity. They also note the continuing expression on the part of some of their respondents that child-rearing is different in these communities than in white communities in Britain.

Waqar Ahmad (1996) in his review of family obligation and social change among Asian communities, suggests that 'behaviour' is negotiated in a complex manner and is influenced by various factors including culture, economic situation, gender, age and 'moral identity', and we should therefore be careful in interpreting any evidence of continuity or change in family relationships and practices. Ahmad concludes that while the situation for the second generation is complex:

> Fears about rejection of the cultural and religious values are not borne out in research studies. On the whole, the second generation shows much continuity with parental traditions, alongside areas of modification. And even where values conflict, as in approaches to marriage, personal values are carefully balanced against the loss of family support. (Ahmad 1996)

What support materials exist for parents of black and minority ethnic teenagers?

The field of parenting support has experienced rapid changes. Smith's review of parenting programmes (1996) found very few working with parents of teenagers. Roker and Coleman's review (1998) showed that provision had grown fairly dramatically in this area, but also identified gaps in knowledge for those working in this field, and, specifically, a lack of information about what research findings said, and difficulties in accessing relevant resources and materials.

Importantly, these reviews have also identified a lack of materials on the subject of working with black and minority ethnic parents. In 1999 the Race Equality Unit (REU) compiled a database of available parenting materials in the UK and found that beyond the work that the Moyenda project[1] was involved in and some localised initiatives, materials and programmes on parenting paid no more than cursory attention to the issue of parenting a black child, and even less to parenting a black teenager. (The Moyenda project was established as part of the Exploring Parenthood project to look at parenting in black and minority ethnic families. It is now resident at Coram Family.)

In addition, the evidence tells us that opportunities to receive support and affirmation of existing coping strategies which alleviate stress and allow parents to provide nurturing environments for their children – as well as opportunities to explore other parenting methods – have not been open to black and minority ethnic families (Butt and Box 1998; Grimshaw and McGuire 1998; Baginsky 1993). However, it is important that the evidence of limited take-up should not be construed as evidence of black and minority ethnic parents rejecting the concept of parental programmes, as there is anecdotal English evidence, as well as quantitative and qualitative American evidence, that black and minority ethnic parents are willing to use them (Utting 1995). Furthermore, these American studies show evidence of how parents and children have benefited from these programmes (Alvey 1994).

The lack of materials on parents of teenagers has been recognised by a range of agencies working in this field, of which the Trust for the Study of Adolescence is just one. The Home Office, in a recent round of Family Support grants, made the issue of parenting teenagers a priority, and indeed also asked applicants to think specifically about the needs of black and minority ethnic communities.

Strengthening Families, Strengthening Communities parent programme: A strategy to support black and minority ethnic parents and teenagers

At the REU we have been working hard to develop strategies to support black and minority ethnic families. One way this is being achieved is through the development of a parenting programme which engages black and minority ethnic parents by addressing issues of ethnicity, culture and spirituality, acknowledging the impact of racism and discrimination, and building on strengths rather than focusing on weaknesses. Like other programmes, it aims to aid development of positive parent–child relationships, help families develop a range of life skills, and help parents find strategies to build self-esteem, self-discipline and social competence in their children. In addition, the programme aims to develop strong ethnic and cultural roots and to increase parents' ability to access community resources.

The 'Strengthening' programme is not targeted only at parents of teenagers. However, there is a range of information, techniques and activities that work particularly well with parents in this situation. In addition, as with other groups-based support, the programme encourages parents to seek support among their peers, and helps to build this, so that it is one of the long-lasting consequences of participating in the programme. As with any parenting difficulties, knowing that there are others in the same position as you lessens isolation.

WHAT TECHNIQUES ARE USED TO SUPPORT PARENTS WITH TEENAGERS?

Running throughout the programme is the 'rites of passage' component. This focuses on helping parents to assist their childrens' development from childhood to adulthood, and is in fact something that has its roots in many minority ethnic cultures.

A feature of any group's rite of passage is training on the roles and responsibilities of being an adult, as well as knowledge of the history and beliefs of a community. Traditionally, it would have been celebrated by the community as a whole, and evidence of such rites exists in many African and Asian communities today. It marks the point when young men and women become adult members of the community and are considered eligible to begin families of their own.

Of course, in the absence of such defining events young people are, in a sense, developing their own. Adulthood is often seen in terms of a legislated adult age, e.g. the age of consent, or as a series of activities, such as drug or alcohol use or engaging in sexual activity, instead of a transition where knowledge and ability must be demonstrated.

The 'Strengthening' programme, then, provides parents with information and activities to assist their children in this transition from childhood to adulthood in the personal, spiritual, physical, mental, cultural, historical, emotional, economic, social and political realms of development. The aim is to help young people develop into socially competent adults. This component of the programme allows parents to gain information on, and to explore, issues that worry them with regard to their teenagers. For example, the physical rite of passage addresses the areas of sexual health, drugs, and alcohol. (A study for Barnardos (1999) identified these issues as being of particular concern for parents when their children reach adolescence.) Parents are given some information on the relationship of drugs and alcohol to health, violence and criminal activity, and are encouraged to explore their concerns and values with other parents in similar positions. A range of suggestions are made as to activities that parents can do with their teenagers to prepare them for the challenges that they will face. As with all of the rites of passage areas, parents are allowed to decide for themselves what is manageable for them in the context of their religious, cultural and ethnic beliefs, rather than have specific methods imposed upon them as the 'right' way of parenting.

The rites of passage components allow parents to explore and gain confidence in dealing with a vast range of issues which impact on their children:

- how to ensure their teenage child has positive role models in his/her life
- how to help young people to have positive, healthy relationships with others
- how to help a child avoid drugs
- how to emphasise the importance of education and get the best for your child from the system
- how to maintain rituals, ceremonies, custom and traditions which are part of your culture
- how to develop respectful relationships across family generations
- how to help young people develop techniques for anger management
- ways in which young people can be encouraged to develop financial responsibility.

In addition, for those who believe it is important for individuals to take responsibility for the community and society and to participate in a democracy, there is an opportunity to explore social and political issues.

Other areas of the programme also address the needs of parents and teenagers. The growing incidence of depression and suicide among adolescents is covered with a discussion on factors associated with this problem, suggestions for ways not to respond, an explorations of myths around depression and suicide, and suggestions for ways to help young people in this situation.

An opportunity is given to parents twice within the programme to explore the issues that worry them most about bringing up children. This means that the programme has a degree of flexibility to meet the needs of each set of parents that most other programmes do not, and this can be particularly useful when working with black and minority ethnic parents, where a degree of flexibility is required. These are called 'community speaker' sessions, where expertise is brought in from outside the group to address a particular set of issues. This can be around how to recognise and help with drug abuse; how to advocate for your child with an institution such as the police, or with schools; an opportunity to explore worries about the growth of gang violence and involvement of young people; or to review what opportunities exist for activities and community involvement of young people in the local area. Because the groups are run in localities where parents share many of the same concerns, it is easy to find common worries that they want to address. These community speaker sessions are also presented in a context where parents have spent time locating useful agencies and individuals in their area that can help them with a range of problems, and have been helped to develop skills to contact these agencies in order to get information or advice which may be useful to them in their particular situation. As a result, parents develop a much more confident attitude to dealing with 'authority' figures and to accessing the help they need to support their children.

A whole range of violence prevention techniques are provided, and these are often particularly relevant to parents of teenagers. For families living in inner-city environments, the growth of gang culture is a worry, as is the growing number of weapons and firearms on the streets. Black and minority ethnic families live in high numbers in areas that have been affected by these developments, and added to this is the disproportionate number of young black people coming into contact with the police and judicial system. Parents want help to find ways of developing young people's skills for managing this reality, and their ability to resist pressure to become involved with violence or illegal activities. Suggestions are provided for anger management techniques, solution building and managing conflict through improved communication methods: such things as exploring the difference between assertive and aggressive communication techniques. Of course, not only are these useful skills for teenagers to develop in terms of negotiating the outside world, but they also help to improve relationships within the home, between siblings and with parents.

Black parents, like others, raise the issue of managing behaviour and how to discipline. This becomes particularly difficult during the teenage years when the roles and boundaries of parents and young people become less clear. Most parenting programmes focus on techniques which have most impact if they are used from early on with children. What is more complex is introducing new methods to older children, particularly teenagers who do not necessarily acknowledge the rights of parents to discipline them. The 'Strengthening' programme suggest a wide range of techniques that parents can utilise and also tries to make them age-specific: while methods of 'attention charting' (giving positive attention to children for a behaviour that the parent wants to see more of) may work with 3–12-year-olds, teenagers are unlikely to respond to it. Young adults are much more likely to respond to methods that offer rewards, or exchange good behaviour for privileges. The programme therefore emphasises that 'responsibility equals privileges', but also that 'freedom equals responsibility'. These more effective methods with teenagers include using incentives and implementing family contracts.

The 'Strengthening' programme also presents some developmental information that encourages parents to think about the process of growth and development. Parents discuss child problem behaviours in terms of the relevant stages of development for the ages of their children. A supplement is provided so that parents can bear in mind what is age appropriate at all times.

Other strategies for support

Programmes to develop parenting skills are not the only way to support families with teenagers. The context in which black and minority ethnic families survive social and economic deprivation and discrimination, as well as the diversity of problems that parents and young people face, demand a range of interventions to support black and minority ethnic families.

Educational support

Because of the disproportionately high level of school exclusion among some black and minority ethnic populations, and worries that the schools are failing black and minority ethnic children, a major concern of many black and minority ethnic parents is helping their child negotiate the education system. This has resulted in a number of projects established specifically to address this problem. One such example is the growth of supplementary schools, such as Kokayi in North London, or the African Caribbean supplementary school in Leamington Spa, which are an additional method of schooling outside school hours (often at the weekend). These are run within a range of settings, including schools, churches and community centres, and are organised and staffed by members of black and minority ethnic communities. Much of the aim has been to help black and minority ethnic children to achieve better in mainstream schooling, but also it provides the opportunity to deliver a wider curriculum where aspects of black history or literature are taught, or for an emphasis to be placed on a particular religious affiliation which some may see as missing from mainstream schooling.

Support for young people experiencing school exclusion has often also developed from within the community in response to the need, and includes helping young black and minority ethnic people access other forms of education, providing support and advice to families when engaging with their child's school over issues of exclusion, and providing advocates to support families.

Work with young offenders or those at risk of offending

Many projects have combined work around education and exclusion with preventative work with young people coming into contact with the criminal justice system, such as Dalston Youth Project (DYP), in Hackney, London, which works with a largely, but not exclusively, black population. They have developed a programme with a range of interventions aimed at alienated young people. Referrals come from various sources, including concerned parents, and although initially the programme was aimed at young people only, it now offers services to parents also, recognising that support needs to be provided for both. The bulk of the service to young people is a mentoring and education programme helping young people to set goals and work towards them. The programme helps to build skills and confidence, as well as providing the opportunities to gain qualifications and to acquire valuable work experience. Alongside this, advice is provided to parents, especially direction to relevant agencies, and an opportunity to participate in a parenting programme (currently this project is providing the 'Strengthening' programme). So far the outcomes of this project have been positive, and a whole series of replica projects based on this model have been established, offering first and foremost support to young socially excluded and alienated people, and also – recognising that in order to support these young people you need to support their parents – support to parents.

Mentoring and peer learning

Alongside many of the educational support projects and work with young offenders, there has been a growth in mentoring schemes, such as those supported by Crime Concern and Divert, and run by agencies such as Westminster Race Equality Council, or Shared Vision in Brixton. These have developed out of the need for positive role models who can offer black and minority ethnic young people advice and suggestions for negotiating the difficult transition from childhood to adulthood – such things as managing peer pressure and avoiding moving towards a life of crime. Mentoring programmes are not always about working with young offenders or those at risk of offending; they have value for a whole range of young people. There has a been a great deal of interest of late in the role these programmes could have in a range of settings, such as raising educational attainment and raising expectations in terms of future plans, as well as possible benefits in terms of lowering involvement in drugs and gang culture, and reducing the rate of teenage pregnancies. Many agencies and institutions, including many schools and community groups, have developed mentoring programmes which aim to provide an alternative adult in whom young people can confide when their relationship with parents is fraught – someone who is not a professional, but can often provide the young person with advice and help in order to solve problems or achieve goals. Many of the mentoring programmes are also moving towards more parental involvement and work with families, acknowledging that parents also need help in dealing with their adolescent children.

Similarly, peer learning programmes aim to disseminate experiences to young people which may encourage them to think about taking particular courses of action, such as getting involved in drugs or crime, or having a child while young. Young people who have experience of these things themselves are used to educate others away from it. An example of this type of work has been carried out by the Naz project in London, which has worked in partnership to train young Asian people around sexual health issues to disseminate information to other young people in a community setting. This has been particularly effective where it has traditionally been hard to facilitate communication between generations or within the family on certain issues.

Engaging black and minority ethnic families

Having a range of services and interventions available to meet the needs of black and minority ethnic families is important. However, the evidence demonstrates that provision of services alone is not enough, and that effectively engaging black and minority ethnic families requires consideration of other issues:

- consultation and involvement of black and minority ethnic communities in identifying needs and in planning and delivering services

- acting on any consultations, so that the process is taken seriously and trust can begin to be established between black and minority ethnic service users and agencies delivering services

- allocating specific resources including money, workers and buildings to work with black and minority ethnic families

- locating services within black and minority ethnic communities

- prioritising outreach as a way to reach out and engage with black and minority ethnic families, particularly newly arrived refugee communities

- working in partnership with the black voluntary sector, such as supplementary schools, and involving faith groups

- building a highly trained, skilled workforce that utilises relevant and non-stereotypical knowledge in working with communities, communicates effectively, is flexible, and respects the families they work with.

(Butt and Box 1998)

Conclusion

The evidence on the experience of black and minority ethnic communities, as a recent report from the SEU (1998) has documented, is that 'ethnic minority groups are more likely than the rest of the population to live in poor areas, be unemployed, have low incomes, live in poor housing, have poor health and be the victims of crime'. The consequences of this for black and minority ethnic families, in particular their ability to cope with crisis, remain largely undocumented. However, the extent of the experience of poverty does suggest that it is a significant stress for black and minority ethnic families, and will no doubt impact on attempts to promote the wellbeing of children and young people. These stresses, combined with those factors, such as a failing education system, that impact disproportionately on black and minority ethnic young people, coming in addition to problems of adolescence, obviously make the process of parenting a black teenager difficult.

This process, however, can be supported. Despite the documented lack of appropriate resources for use with black and minority ethnic families, a range of initiatives is taking place to improve the situation, such as projects supported by the Home Office Family Support grant to make existing materials and mainstream organisations more accessible to black and minority ethnic families and those working with them, and, as seen in this chapter, the development of the Strengthening Families Parenting Programme. The programme adopts the classic model of supporting parents in developing relationships and methods of discipline which support self-esteem and social competence, while counteracting violence within families and the community. What appears to us unique in this programme is the method of engagement, which includes exploration of the origins of individuals' parenting styles through their ethnicity, religion and gender; emphasis on dealing with whole human beings (mental, physical, emotional and spiritual); and seeing parenting not as an individual responsibility, but as part of the whole community.

As also shown, resources to support black and minority ethnic families with teenagers need to include more than parenting programmes as they need to address the context in which parenting takes place. There is a need for interventions that cover education, health and youth offending, and that do so by working with parents and carers alongside young people. Finally, engaging effectively with black and ethnic minority families necessitates understanding the experience of black communities and developing skills around communication, being flexible, and building respect and trust. It is this combination of holistic services designed to meet the specific needs of black and minority ethnic families and young people, provided by workers skilled in engaging these communities, that will ensure that the needs of black and minority families are effectively met.

References

Ahmad, W. (1996) 'Family obligation and community care.' In W. Ahmad and K. Atkin (eds) 'Race' and Community Care. Milton Keynes: Open University Press.

Ahmed, S. (1986) 'Cultural racism in work with Asian women and girls' in S. Ahmed, J. Cheetham and J. Small (eds). Social Work with Black Children and their Families. London: BT Batsford.

Alvey, K. (1994) Parent Training Today: A Social Necessity. California: Centre for the Improvement of Child Caring.

Amin, K. and Oppenheim, C. (1992) Poverty in Black and White. London: Child Poverty Action Group/Runnymede Trust.

Arnold, E. (1988) 'Cross-cultural aspects of physical abuse.' Child Abuse Review 2, 1, 31–33. London: BASCPAN.

Baginsky, M. (1993) Parent Link in Waltham Forest: An Evaluation. London: Baginsky Associates for Waltham Forest LEA.

Barn, R. (1993) Black Children in the Public Care System. London: Batsford.

Barn, R., Sinclair, R. and Ferdinand, D. (1997) Acting on Principle. BAAF.

Barnardos (1999) Attitudes Towards Parenting. London: Prepared by NDI Families on behalf of Barnardos.

Barter, C. (1999) Protecting Children from Racism and Racial Abuse: A Research Review. London: NSPCC.

Berthoud, R. (1997) The Income of Ethnic Minorities. London: PSI.

Berthoud, R. (1999) Young Caribbean Men and the Labour Market. York: YPS.

Black Labour Market News (2000) 'New Deal and Ethnic Minority Participants.' Issue 6/7, May 2000, 36–40.

Butt, J. (2000) 'Race equality: Caribbean young men.' In Research Matters 9, April–October 2000.

Butt, J. and Box, L. (1998) Family Centred: A Study of the Use of Family Centres by Black Families. London: Race Equality Unit.

Childline (1997) Children and Racism. London: Childline.

Coleman, J. (1999) Key Data on Adolescence. Trust for the Study of Adolescence.

Coleman, J. (2000) 'Young people in Britain at the beginning of a new century.' Children and Society 14.

Commission for Racial Equality (1996) We Regret to Inform You: Testing for Racial Discrimination in Youth Employment in the North of England and Scotland. London: Commission for Racial Equality.

Dosnajh, J. and Ghuman, P. (1997) 'Child-rearing practices of two generations of Punjabi parents.' Children and Society 11, pp.29–43.

Gillborn and Gipps (1996) Recent Research on the Achievement of Ethnic Minority Pupils. HMSO for Ofsted.

Grimshaw, R. and McGuire, C. (1998) Evaluating Parenting Programmes: A Study of Stakeholders' Views. London: NCB.

Haskey, J. (1996) 'Population Review (6): Families and households in Great Britain.' Population Trends No 85, London: HMSO.

Hylton, C. (1997) Family Survival Strategies. Exploring Parenthood. York: Joseph Rowntree Foundation.

Office for National Statistics (1996) *Social Focus on Ethnic Minorities*. London: HMSO.

Office for National Statistics (1998) *Social Trends 28*. London: The Stationery Office.

Roker, D. and Coleman, J. (1998) '"Parenting Teenagers" programmes: A UK perspective.' *Children and Society* 12, 359–372.

Small, J. (1982) 'New black families.' *Adoption and Fostering 6*, 3, 35–39. London: BAAF.

Smith, C. (1996) *Developing Parenting Programmes*. London: NCB.

Social Exclusion Unit (1998) *Bringing Britain Together: A National Strategy for Neighbourhood Renewal*. London: The Stationery Office.

Social Exclusion Unit (1999) *Teenage Pregnancy*. London: The Stationery Office.

Social Exclusion Unit (2000) *Minority Ethnic Issues in Social Exclusion and Neighbourhood Renewal*. London: The Stationery Office.

Utting D. (1995) 'Family and parenthood: supporting families, preventing breakdown: a guide to the debate.' York: Joseph Rowntree Foundation.

Chapter 4

Parenting and Youth Crime

Clem Henricson

Introduction

The influence of parenting on the behaviour of young people has been one of the principal incentives for government investment in support for parents during the teenage years. Adolescence is the age when most crime is committed, and parents provide one of the main resources for controlling young people whose behaviour has got out of hand. They have a legal responsibility to care for their child, and legislation by successive governments has reflected the view that parents should be responsible for preventing their children from committing delinquent acts. For example, the Criminal Justice Act (1991) sought to punish parents by introducing bind-overs whereby parents stand to lose a considerable amount of money if they fail to exert sufficient care and control over their children. Subsequently, the Crime and Disorder Act (1999) took a more supportive approach through the establishment of the Parenting Order, which enables courts to require parents of young offenders to take part in parenting classes.

As a backdrop to the Parenting Order, there has also been major investment in the infrastructure of support for parents of adolescents through the Youth Justice Board's development fund for parenting provision, and the Family Policy Unit's grants programme targeting parents of teenagers. Indeed, taking a proactive stance on crime prevention, the Home Office has been at the core of the present government's emphasis on holistic family support, which has included, among other initiatives, the establishment of the National Family and Parenting Institute.

Few would doubt the inherent value in providing proper backup for parents. Parenting is a difficult task done for free, and society has its duty. But can investment in parenting services and, in particular, support for the parents of teenagers be justified in terms of crime prevention? In this chapter we consider the research evidence base, and conclude that, by and large, it can. While peer-group pressures and youth unemployment undoubtedly have a large part to play, the evidence shows that the impact of parenting on youth crime is highly significant. Nevertheless, there are limitations on the capacity of both parents and parenting interventions to effect change, and these need to be recognised, particularly in the development of support programmes that have as their main aim the modification of young people's behaviour.

We examine the parenting practices which are most strongly associated with delinquent development, and go on to look, in particular, at:

- the impact of violence and harsh, erratic discipline

- the role of family disruption

- the effect that having criminal parents can have

- the negative implications of neglect and lack of supervision

- the importance of emotional attachment between parent and child.

We examine underlying economic influences. We consider the nature of 'positive parenting', and the significance of support for this type of parenting as a means of protecting young people from becoming involved in crime. The chapter concludes on a cautionary note with a discussion of different patterns of delinquent development and their relative susceptibility to change though parenting interventions.

Parenting practices

The relationship between parenting practices and delinquent development has been the subject of much criminological research. One of the principal meta-analyses of this literature is Loeber and Stouthamer-Loeber's (1986) assessment of British, American and Scandinavian studies, which points to four parenting approaches which have been found to have a causal relationship with the development of delinquency in young people. They are:

- neglect and a failure to supervise effectively
- conflict between parent and child, which involves chronic disobedience by the child and failure on the part of the parent to exert control in a consistent, nonaggressive way
- parental criminality
- family disruption, particularly where there is emotional disturbance and conflict between the parents.

One of the best known and well reputed longitudinal studies of criminality, *The Cambridge Study of Delinquent Development* (Farrington and West 1990) produced similar findings demonstrating that young people were more likely to become involved in crime if, as children and adolescents, they were subjected to one or a combination of the following – harsh or erratic discipline, emotional or physical neglect, or inadequate supervision. The study also showed that parents' deviant behaviour often predicated delinquent development and recidivism in their children; this finding was subsequently corroborated by research undertaken by Hagell and Newburn (1996).

Violence and harsh, erratic discipline

Numerous studies have shown the negative impact of excessive and abusive physical punishment on the emotional and mental wellbeing of young people, with one of the principal outcomes being an increased risk of delinquent development involving violence and aggression (Farrington 1994). Through their review of cross-sectional and prospective studies, Hawkins, Catalano and Miller (1992) have also demonstrated a link between physical punishment and conduct problems, and Thompson's (2000) meta-analysis of some 88 studies of physical punishment concluded that, although children may comply with the command associated with the punishment, in the longer term there are serious negative effects including 'increased aggression in the child as well as more antisocial and criminal behaviour in childhood and adulthood…'

Some commentators have suggested that the role of the young person's character may not be fully recognised by this analysis, and that the relationship between punishment and negative behaviour may not be causal at all, but may instead be dependent on a correlation with other influences. Adolescents with conduct problems may, for instance, have fewer social skills, making it more difficult for them to maintain appropriate interactions with their parents. Furthermore, there may be other complications involving age, gender, socio-economic status, or parental problems such as mental illness, sociopathy or conflict (Henricson and Gray, forthcoming).

However, a recent review of literature in this field by Leach (1999) suggests that the use of physical punishment by parents does have a negative impact on young people's behavioural problems which is independent of other variables (Straus and Paschall 1998; Gunnoe and Mariner 1997; Straus, Sugarman and Giles-Sims 1997; Brezina 1998). These American studies of nationally representative samples of children, involving measurements of antisocial behaviour over two years, found that where physical punishment was used, levels of antisocial behaviour increased, regardless of the initial behavioural characteristics of the child. Furthermore this tendency held good regardless of race, socio-economic status, gender of the child and relationship with parents (Straus and Paschall 1998).

Family disruption

A considerable body of research has pointed to the impact of family disruption on delinquent development. Wells and Rankin (1991) in their meta-analysis of 50 American and European studies in this area found that young people growing up in broken homes were 10–15 per cent more likely to become involved in crime than those coming from homes with two natural parents. They also ran an even higher risk of truancy, running away from home and underage drinking.

A number of analyses have suggested that it is not the absence of one parent from the home, *per se*, which is responsible for these negative outcomes, rather it is interparental conflict and/or the absence of parental warmth which have the principal adverse effect. For example, in their examination of longitudinal research in Great Britain and the US, Cherlin *et al.* (1991) showed that marital discord increases the likelihood of delinquent development regardless of whether the parents separate. In *The Cambridge Study of Delinquent Development* separations (usually from the father) caused by parental conflict were found to predict criminality, but not those caused by death or hospitalisation. In this research, 32 per cent of boys from homes separated by parental conflict were convicted as juveniles, compared with 20 per cent of those where the cause was death or hospitalisation and 16 per cent of boys from intact homes (Farrington 1994). In her study of serious offending by boys, McCord (1982) found that offending rates were high for those from unbroken homes with high levels of conflict

(52%) compared with a low prevalence rate (22%) for those from broken homes with affectionate mothers.

Loeber and Stouthamer-Loeber (1986) in their meta-analysis found that, while family disruption contributed significantly to the likelihood of criminal behaviour in young people, it was less potent than the other contributory factors. They attributed this to the possibility that, while the effective socialising of children was often disrupted because of the stress being experienced by the family during separation, the basic socialising skills of the parent remained intact, to be resumed when the crisis was resolved, or at least ameliorated.

Criminal parents

Intergenerational transmission of criminality is widely recognised as a strong predictor of youth crime. In her Birmingham study, Harriet Wilson (1980, 1987) found that 45 per cent of sons of offending parents were convicted or cautioned, as compared with 19 per cent of those whose parents did not have a criminal record. The *Cambridge Study* showed that under five per cent of the 400 subject families were responsible for about half of their criminal convictions (West and Farrington 1977). The Cambridge researchers found that, unlike other precursors of delinquency, criminal parents were linked to later, rather than early onset of offending, and that there was also a greater tendency for the offending to last through into adulthood, with a high level of recidivism.

The mechanics linking criminality across generations have been the subject of different interpretations. Mednick, Gabrielli and Hutchings (1984) have suggested a genetic influence through their examination of adopted children in Denmark. This study showed that children adopted as infants were more likely to offend if one of their natural parents had been a criminal than if one of their adoptive parents was one. There has, however, been some suggestion that this study may have been methodologically flawed because of a failure to take account of the selection process whereby the children were allocated to particular adoptive parents (Walters and White 1989). Moving to an interpretation based on nurture, Loeber and Stouthamer-Loeber (1986) concluded that parents' deviant behaviour and attitudes were being transmitted because they failed to label misbehaviour as wrong, condoned the settlement of playground disputes by fighting, and were protective of their children when they were found to be behaving antisocially by neighbours or the police. Farrington (1994), on the other hand, noted that 89 per cent of criminal fathers in the *Cambridge Study* were critical of youth offending and did not want their sons to offend. He considered that the most plausible explanation was the poor supervision exercised by criminal parents. Laub and Sampson's (1988) analysis of data collated by Glueck showed that criminal fathers were more inclined to use harsh and erratic discipline, and they also demonstrated that mothers with a criminal history often failed to supervise their children effectively.

Neglect and lack of supervision

Neglect and lack of supervision has been identified in Loeber and Stouthamer-Loeber's meta-analysis as the greatest risk factor associated with delinquency, although the other negative influences, as we have seen, are potent. For example, in her research in Boston, McCord (1979) showed that failure to supervise was the strongest predictor of violence and property crimes, and Robins (1978), in her longitudinal follow-up studies in St Louis, found a consistent link with later offending. In a working-class district in the UK, Harriet Wilson (1980, 1987) examined the role of supervision for 10–11-year-old boys in the context of different measures of what she described as 'social handicap', including school contact and attendance, school clothing, economic status and family size. The aspects of supervision assessed included time and activities away from home, unsupervised time on the streets and rules concerning homecoming. Using self report and parental and teacher ratings of antisocial behaviour at school and in the community, Wilson found that there was a direct relationship between poor supervision and misbehaviour, and that this existed independently of social disadvantage. Lax supervision was found to be a strong predictor not only of initial involvement in crime, but also of repeat offending. Riley and Shaw (1985) have also demonstrated that, in communities experiencing social deprivation, the capacity of parents to supervise their children was the critical protective factor preventing young people from becoming involved in crime. A number of studies have shown that children in receipt of neglectful parenting suffer most in terms of their psychological development and are at greatest risk not only of delinquency, but also of related behaviours such as drug and alcohol abuse (Maccoby and Martin 1983; Steinberg 1990).

With the strength of the association between poor supervision and criminality, it is pertinent to consider current trends in parental control. The evidence suggests that there has been a considerable decline in levels of parental supervision in recent years. Felson and Gottfredson (1984) and Junger-Tas and Terlouw (1991) conducted similar surveys of people's experiences of supervision when they were aged 17, asking questions relating to time spent with family activities and deadlines for returning home. A marked decline in supervision was found. The turning point appears to have been in the 1960s, prior to when teenagers spent considerably more of their time in the company of their parents both in and outside the home. After 1960, young people were returning home later, 30 per cent after 2 am., and their mobility had increased substantially, with one third spending Saturday nights away from their home town, thus being unsupervised in anonymous environments. Junger Tas (1994) has attributed rises in delinquency among young people to this loss of parental control.

How, then, might parental supervision of young people be improved from a social crime prevention perspective? Gottfredson and Hirschi (1990) have recommended consistent monitoring of the young person's behaviour, recognising deviant behaviour and applying discipline when it occurs. Patterson's (1980) well-evaluated coercion model, which comprises a successful training formula for parents who are experiencing problems in managing their children's behaviour, makes similar recommendations. However, Coleman (1997) has identified the importance of adopting a sensitive and not too intrusive approach when monitoring the activities of adolescents. A right to some degree of privacy and autonomy is crucial at this stage in a young person's development. This view is supported by a number of studies which emphasise the necessity of enhancing communication and responding flexibly to the increasing socio-cognitive powers of adolescents in order to reduce unnecessary conflict and adverse peer pressure, and so as to develop young people's sense of personal responsibility (Brown and Mann 1990; Fuligini and Eccles 1993; Holmbeck, Paikoff and Brooks-Gunn 1995). The relevance of this analysis to preventing youth crime can be seen in the results of Wells and Rankin's (1988) survey of a national sample of 15–17-year-old boys, which found that too much, as well as too little, parental control predicated delinquency; a moderate level of strictness was the approach which was required to minimise young people's involvement in crime.

Attachment and communication

As well as being influenced by stress factors, such as poverty and family disruption, the capacity of an individual parent to supervise his or her child will largely be determined by the level of attachment and emotional bond between them. Riley and Shaw (1985) examined the impact of the parent–child relationship on parents' ability to supervise, and found that young people who engaged in criminal activity were less willing than others to accept parental control. A positive relationship between parent and child was a prerequisite for the provision of effective supervision, and where this did not exist, parents had difficulty in controlling their children. Grove and Crutchfield (1982) in their survey of 600 parents, including a cross-section of black and white interviewees, found that where there was a poor emotional relationship between parent and child, where they did not get along well together, then supervision was seriously undermined. Parents' negative feelings towards their children were also strong predictors of future criminality.

Examining the issue from the perspective of preventing delinquency, Cernkovich and Giordano (1987) surveyed the impact of family relationships on 824 young people. They considered, alongside supervision, matters relating to acceptance and respect, caring and trust, intimate communication associated with thoughts and feelings, instrumental communication concerned with practical issues, conflict and parental disapproval of peers. Effective intimate and instrumental communication, evidencing high levels of attachment, were found to have a significant influence in preventing young people from becoming involved in crime. Van Voorhis *et al.* (1988) reached similar conclusions in their research, which established affection and supervision as highly pertinent factors inhibiting the emergence of offending behaviour. Laub and Sampson's (1988) research showed that not only was parental emotional rejection of children highly correlated with children's delinquent development, but it was also associated with patterns of persistent and serious offending. Of course, rejection between parent and child can work two ways and is interdependent, so not surprisingly Johnson (1987), for example, found that children who had seriously negative feelings towards their parents were also more prone to delinquency.

Parental gender and attachment
Some studies have examined the differences in the impact of mothers and fathers on young people's behaviour, linking this with the issue of attachment. A substantial body of evidence has demonstrated that mothers are the principal influence in children's lives and that this extends beyond early

childhood through to adolescence. They spend more time and are more closely involved with their children during the teenage years than men are (Paulson and Sputa 1996). Mothers are closer to both their sons and their daughters, supporting them, having a broader range of communication with them and being more aware of the developmental changes which their children are experiencing (Collins and Russell 1991; Youmiss and Smollar 1985). However, they may also experience more conflict because of this closeness (Collins and Russell 1991).

While fathers may have a more formal, less intimate relationship with children, both before and during adolescence, than mothers do, some research has suggested that they have a significant part to play in helping young people adjust to and grow into adulthood, and that this has an important impact on behavioural outcomes (Wagner, Cohen and Brook 1996; Shulman and Seiffge-Krenke 1997). Johnson's (1987) research involving 734 high school pupils, which addressed issues such as trust, respect and attachment, found, like other studies, that children of both sexes were more attached to their mother. However, on examining the link with offending, the data revealed that a close bond between father and child, particularly between father and son, was more influential than the mother–child relationship in preventing the development of delinquency, and Junger-Tas (1994) has commented that this indicates a role for fathers relating to norm setting, discipline and control.

On the other hand, McCord's (1982) analysis of offending by boys in Boston found maternal attachment to be a major protective factor. She recorded low levels of offending by young people from broken homes where there was an affectionate mother. Commenting on the data, Farrington (1994) has suggested that it shows 'that a loving mother might in some sense be able to compensate for the loss of a father' (p.11).

Economic influences

Both recorded crime and longitudinal research studies have shown that young people from families experiencing economic deprivation are more prone to offending than those from more affluent backgrounds. Wadsworth (1979) in the *National Health and Development Survey* in the UK found that sons of fathers who were the least skilled and educated manual workers received more convictions for serious offending than others. Within the sample of working-class boys in the *Cambridge Study*, young men aged 18 from the poorest households were twice as likely to be convicted of an offence as those from families with an adequate income, and there was an even stronger correlation with recidivism (West 1982; West and Farrington 1973).

The possibility has been mooted that young people from disadvantaged backgrounds tend to be prosecuted by the police for reasons other than their higher levels of offending. While this may offer a partial explanation, evidence from self and third-party report studies also shows trends supporting the thesis that relative deprivation is associated with delinquent development. For example, in the national cohort which is the subject of the *Child Health and Education Study*, Osborn, Butler and Morris (1984) found a strong association between pre-school children with behavioural problems and relative deprivation. In their overviews of research, Junger-Tas (1994) and Rutter, Giller and Hagell (1998) have noted the tendency for children with early chronic behavioural problems to come from socially disadvantaged backgrounds. Elliot and Huizinga (1983), in their assessment of self-report studies, have demonstrated a link between social disadvantage and serious youth offending, involving, for example, burglary and violence rather than status offences, such as drug and alcohol misuse and rowdiness.

There is, then, a broadly accepted association between family income and youth offending, but how that association operates is a separate question. In their reviews of research, Utting, Bright and Henricson (1993) and Junger Tas (1994) have concluded that the principal mechanism is through the stress that is placed on parents by adverse economic and situational circumstances which make it difficult for them to supervise their children effectively. They point to the findings of Harriet Wilson's (1980, 1987) study of the relationship between 'social handicap' and supervision.

In Wilson's research into boys' outcomes, she found that lax supervision increased with higher levels of social disadvantage. However, some parents increased their levels of supervision to counteract the negative influences of a disadvantaged neighbourhood, and this enabled Wilson to see that there was not a direct causal relationship between poverty and juvenile offending. She found instead that supervision was the significant factor, with both deprivation and youth crime being correlated with inadequate supervision.

Larzelere and Patterson (1990) confirmed this finding in their longitudinal clinical studies of boys and their families at the Oregon Social Learning Center. They found that the relationship between socio-economic status and juvenile offending was mediated by parents' child behaviour management practices. These practices encompassed not only supervision, but also the degree to which parents exerted consistent, moderate discipline.

Pertinent, too, are the issues raised by Kagitcibasi (1996) in relation to parents' levels of education. Inadequate education is often both a contributory cause and a consequence of economic stress, and Kagitcibasi has suggested that parents who have education deficits are less able to use moderate discipline practices which depend on a relatively high level of verbal facility.

Positive parenting

Having examined the negative influences of certain parenting practices on the behaviour of young people, it is important, in order to develop support systems for families, to establish the type of parenting style we should be promoting to maximise parents' capacity to protect their children from delinquency. In child development circles, the generally preferred model of parenting is known as *authoritative parenting*. This style involves the giving of warmth and affection, which is necessary to enhance the young person's sense of self-worth and ability to interact with other people. It requires a reasonable level of *demandingness*, linked with effective discipline; this is crucial to developing the child/young person's sense of social responsibility and ability to exert self-control. It is also important, particularly as children grow into young adults, that there is respect for their individuality and right to develop and communicate their views; often termed *psychological autonomy*, this is needed to enable young people to gradually assume independence and to be sufficiently competent to do so. (Baumrind 1967; Hill 1980; Maccoby and Martin 1983). Paikoff and Brooks-Gunn (1991) have described positive strategies here whereby 'adolescents gradually take on more responsibility for managing their own activities under a watchful parental gaze'.

The authoritative parenting style has been found to work well for one- and two-parent families, and for families from a variety of social and economic backgrounds (Shucksmith, Hendry and Glendenning 1995). It is widely recognised, however, that more research is needed to establish how it should be applied in respect of a range of ethnic groups (Dornbusch *et al.* 1987). This research will need to take into account cross-cultural studies which suggest that while the universal requirements of good parenting are affection coupled with effective discipline, the appropriateness of that discipline depends to a considerable extent on the norms of the society in which the child is being brought up (Kagitcibasi 1996). Thus, in a society where conformity is a desired outcome, a high level of parental control may be appropriate (Peisner 1989; Sinha 1981; Bond 1986). Furthermore, there is evidence to suggest that failure to provide discipline which conforms to a society's norms, whatever those norms may be, may result in a young person feeling rejected. Trommsdorf (1985) has found that in Japan, lack of strong discipline of a young person will often be interpreted as rejection, whereas in an individualistic society such as the US, where greater adolescent freedom is the norm, too much control is a token of rejection. A formulation for authoritative parenting is required which accommodates this degree of variation.

Support programmes

Perhaps one of the clearest indications of the role of parenting in preventing delinquent development can be seen from the beneficial effects on young people's behaviour which have accrued from parenting interventions. A number of significant programmes specifically designed for the families of young people with behavioural difficulties have been fully evaluated for behavioural outcomes in the US. They range from self-directed to highly intensive family therapy interventions.

Parenting Wisely. Parenting Wisely is a self-directed CD-ROM, cognitive-behavioural parenting education package which has been used successfully in respect of youth justice court orders in the US. An evaluation of the programme with parents whose children had been involved in the juvenile court or children's services has demonstrated increased use of the parenting skills taught in the programme and a reduction in children's problem behaviours. Clinically significant reductions in problem behaviours were found in half the participants, with most parents reporting at least moderate improvements. A control group assigned to standard treatment, usually probation for adolescents, showed no improvement over the same six-month post-treatment period (Gordon and Kacir 1997).

Multisystemic Therapy. In contrast with the self-directed nature of Parenting Wisely, multisystemic therapy is an intensive therapeutic approach working holistically in home- or community-based settings with families who are experiencing serious difficulties. Evaluations show favourable results, including reduced behavioural problems, a reduction in offending, and improved family relations, with a higher rate of positive outcomes than control groups using standard diversionary services and individual counselling (Borduin *et al.* 1995; Henggeler, Melton and Smith 1992; Henggeler 1999).

Oregon Social Learning Centre (OSLC). Gerald Patterson and his colleagues have undertaken parenting education and therapeutic work with young people at risk of, or experiencing, behavioural difficulties for a number of years. Many of the young people treated are delinquent and come from seriously dysfunctional families. While enhanced communication and negotiation is a feature, the main focus of Patterson's 'coercion model' is behaviour modification. Significantly, success rates for the OSLC model are far higher for children under the age of 10 than for older age groups. A 75 per cent success rate with children aged 0–9 has been found, compared with only a 25 per cent success rate with adolescents. The reason given for this is the reduced influence of parents and enhanced influence of peers during adolescence. It may also be that the programme's emphasis on a behavioural response is less appropriate for teenagers, and that for this group more consideration needs to be given to communication issues (Patterson 1982; Patterson and Forgatch 1987; Patterson and Narrett 1990; Patterson 1994).

Patterns in delinquent development

In developing support programmes it is essential to recognise that there are not only a number of aspects of parenting which may be determining, or contributing to, young people's behavioural problems; there are also different types of delinquent development. The review by Rutter *et al.* (1998) of delinquency in young people produced a classification of principal types of juvenile offending, with the main dividing line in terms of outcomes and support requirements coming between cases where offending starts in early childhood (early onset) and offending which starts later, during the young person's teens.

Early onset offending, which is linked to socio-cognitive problems, is the most difficult to address. It has the most serious outcomes, certainly in terms of persistence (Loeber, Keenan and Zhang 1997). It escalates during adolescence, and often continues into adulthood, forming a category of offenders described as 'life course persistent'. In their analysis of a longitudinal survey in Stockholm, Stattin and Magnusson (1996) found this type of offending to be associated with recidivism and to account for some 60 per cent of offences. Although the findings are not fully established, the longitudinal analysis by Moffit *et al.* (1996) suggests that this life course persistent group comprises about six per cent of the general population.

Antisocial behaviour which leads to early onset offending may arise even before school age. Moffit *et al.* found that this group exhibited characteristics such as inattention, restlessness and negative behaviour as early as three years of age. Many of these early onset offenders suffer from hyperactivity. This limits a child's attention span and is associated with a range of persistent, reinforcing social deficits, including cognitive difficulties, social malfunctioning, poor relations with peers and antisocial behaviour, ranging from conflict with authority to violence and property misdemeanours (Loeber *et al.* 1997; Stattin and Magnusson (1996); Rutter *et al.* 1998). In terms of causation, Rutter and his colleagues have noted that there is considerable genetic influence in determining hyperactivity, making intervention in this area particularly difficult. Nevertheless, there are indications that parenting support can be of value if introduced in the early stages before the child's behaviour patterns become entrenched. Medication can help to remedy hyperactivity, and Campbell (1997) has shown that positive parenting can result in improved outcomes for these children by the time they reach adolescence. The sample used by Moffit *et al.* (1996) also has examples of 'recovered' children.

In contrast to early onset offending, Rutter and his colleagues found that offending which begins in adolescence is generally not sustained through into adulthood. Most offenders during the teenage years fall within this category. Studies suggest that there is no association with hyperactivity for these young people and little evidence that they relate poorly to peers or are unable to function effectively socially. During early childhood they tend to be temperamentally similar to those who do not become involved with crime, and do not exhibit antisocial behaviour (Moffit *et al.* 1996). This type of offending arises during the teenage years, often as a product of problems associated with adolescent development. The role of the parent–child relationship is clearly relevant here, and there is consequently considerable scope for parent support programmes to have an impact, although the counter-influence of peer group pressure should be acknowledged.

Conclusion: The role of support services

From the evidence drawn together here, it is clear that parenting has a pervasive influence on the behavioural patterns of young people and on their propensity to commit crimes. Discipline practices that are immoderate and inconsistent, unproductive conflict between parent and child, and between parents themselves, lack of parental affection, neglect and failure to supervise, are all features of parenting which contribute to an increased risk of delinquency. There is, then, a substantial argument to be made for providing multilayered support facilities to enhance parents' capacity to manage their children's behaviour.

Evaluations have demonstrated that parenting programmes can reduce levels of youth offending. Nevertheless, programmes do face difficulties in effecting change, and these limitations need to be recognised. They include matters such as the difficulty of influencing the level of affection and attachment which develops between parent and child, particularly as a consequence of the reciprocal, two-way nature of the parent–child relationship. Negative peer-group influences can be reduced by enhancing supervision and the emotional influence of parents, but they nevertheless remain a potent force which it is difficult for parenting programmes to deal with. The habitual nature of parental responses, such as the use of certain types of punishment, some of which may have been passed down from previous generations, may also be hard to modify. Breaking an intergenerational cycle of criminality will pose major problems, particularly if deviant attitudes are permeating the family ethos, as is suggested to be often the case in Loeber and Stouthamer-Loeber's (1986) meta-analysis. Poverty and the stress caused by personal and neighbourhood deprivation undermine parents' capacity to parent effectively, but parenting support services will not be able to address this type of extraneous factor, other than through lobbying or forming a part of a wider government programme to tackle social deprivation. Limitations such as these need to be confronted in order to develop facilities that are realistic in their anticipated outcomes and which target investment effectively.

The range of facilities offered should reflect the complexity of the relationship between parenting and young people's behaviour. It is also important to ascertain in each case the nature of the issue which is affecting a particular family and to respond accordingly. Different types of programme will be needed. For example, in early onset cases, where there are often serious cognitive and social problems, it may be necessary to provide intensive therapeutic interventions, addressing the family's problems in the round following the multisystemic family therapy model. On the other hand, where offending starts later during the young person's teens as a consequence, say, of adolescent communication difficulties and the use of inappropriate discipline, and is less likely to become deeply entrenched, then a self-directed facility such as the Parenting Wisely CD-ROM may be sufficient.

This overview gives an indication of the volume of research which has been undertaken into the relationship between parenting and youth crime. Not only is the scale of the literature large, the breadth of issues examined is extensive, encompassing the roles of attachment, discipline and supervision, issues relating to intergenerational transmission, culture and gender, and the impact of social disadvantage. Drawing the findings together from a positive perspective, they provide a guide to parenting as a protective agent against delinquent development. Used sensitively, and in a way which genuinely reflects the diverse nature of the relationship between upbringing and criminality, they could make a useful contribution to the development of parenting facilities with a social crime prevention dimension.

References

Baumrind, D. (1967) 'Child care practices anteceding three patterns of pre-school behavior.' *Genetic Psychology Monographs 75*, 43–88.

Bond, M. H. (ed) (1986) *The Psychology of the Chinese People*. Hong Kong: Oxford University Press.

Borduin, C., Mann, B., Cone, L., Hengeller, S., Fucci, B., Blaske, D. and Williams, R. (1995) 'Multisystemic treatment of serious juvenile offenders: long term prevention of criminality and violence.' *Journal of Consulting and Clinical Psychology 63*, 569–78.

Brezina, T. (1998) 'Adolescent maltreatment and delinquency: the question of intervening processes'. *Journal of Research in Crime and Delinquency 35*, 1, 71–99.

Brown, J. and Mann, L. (1990) 'The relationship between family structure and process variable and adolescent decision making.' *Journal of Adolescence 13*, 25–37.

Campbell, S. B. (1997) 'Behaviour problems in preschool children. Developmental and family issues.' In T. O. Ollendick and R. J. Prinz (eds) *Advances in Clinical Child Psychology 19*,1–26. NewYork: Plenum.

Cernkovich, S. and Giordano, P. (1987) 'Family relationships and delinquency.' *Criminology 25*, 2, 295–319.

Cherlin, A., Furstenburg, R., Chase-Lansdale, P., Kiernan, R., Robins, P., Ruane Morrison, D. and Teitler, J. (1991) 'Longitudinal studies of the effects of divorce on children in Great Britain and the United States.' *Science 252*, 7 June 1991 1386–1389.

Coleman, J. (1997) 'The parenting of adolescents in Britain today.' *Children and Society 11*, 44–52.

Collins, W. and Russell, G. (1991) 'Mother–child and father–child relationships in middle childhood and adolescence: a developmental analysis.' *Developmental Review 11*, 99–136.

Dornbusch, S., Ritter, P., Liederman, P., Roberts, D. and Fraleigh, M. (1987) 'The relation of parenting style to adolescent school performance.' *Child Development 58*, 1244–1257.

Elliott, D. and Huizinga, D. (1983) 'Social class and delinquent behaviour in a national youth panel.' *Criminology 21*, 2, 149–177.

Farrington, D. (1994) 'The influences of the family on delinquent development.' In C. Henricson (ed) *Crime and the Family Conference Report*. London: Family Policy Studies Centre.

Farrington, D. and West, D. (1990) 'The Cambridge study in delinquent development: a long-term follow-up of 411 London males.' In G. Kaiser and H. Kerner (eds) *Criminality: Personality, Behaviour, Life History*. Berlin: Springer-Verlag.

Felson, M. and Gottfredson, M. (1984) 'Social indicators of adolescent activities near peers and parents.' *Journal of Marriage and the Family*, August issue, 709–714.

Fuligini, A. and Eccles, J. (1993) 'Perceived parent–child relationships and early adolescents' orientation towards peers.' *Developmental Psychology 29*, 622–632.

Gordon, D. and Kacir, C. (1997) 'Effectiveness of an interactive parent training program for changing behavior for court referred parents.' Website abstract.

Gottfredson, M. and Hirschi, T. (1990) *A General Theory of Crime*. Stanford, California: Stanford University Press.

Grove, W. and Crutchfield, R. (1982) 'The family and juvenile delinquency.' *The Sociological Quarterly 23*, 301–319.

Gunnoe, M. and Mariner, C. (1997) 'Towards a developmental-contextual model of the effects of spanking on children's aggression.' *Archives of Paediatrics and Adolescent Medicine 151*, 768–775.

Hagell, A. and Newburn, T. (1996) 'Family and social contexts of adolescent re-offenders.' *Journal of Adolescence 19*, 5–118.

Hawkins, J. D., Catalano, R. F. and Miller, J. Y. (1992) Risk and protective factors for alcohol and other drug problems in adolescence and early adulthood: Implications for substance abuse prevention. *Psychological Bulletin 112*, 64–105.

Henggeler, S. (1999) 'Multisystemic therapy: An overview of clinical procedures, outcomes and policy implications.' *Child Psychology and Psychiatry Review 4*, 2–10.

Henggeler, S., Melton, G. and Smith L. (1992) 'Family preservation using multisystemic therapy: An effective alternative to incarcerating serious juvenile offenders.' *Journal of Consulting and Clinical Psychology 60*, 953–961.

Henricson C. and Gray, A. (forthcoming) *An Overview of Child Discipline Practices*. London: National Family and Parenting Institute.

Hill, J. P. (1980) 'The family.' In: M. Johnson (ed) *Towards Adolescence: The Middle School Years* (National Society for the Study of Education Yearbook 79). Chicago: Chicago University Press.

Holmbeck, G., Paikoff, R. and Brooks-Gunn, J. (1995) 'Parenting adolescents.' In M. Bornstein (ed) *Handbook of Parenting 1*, Mahwah, NJ: Laurence Erlbaum.

Johnson, R. (1987) 'Mothers' versus fathers' role in causing delinquency.' *Adolescence 22*, 86.

Junger-Tas, J. (1994) 'The changing family and its relationship with delinquent behaviour.' In C. Henricson (ed) *Crime and the Family Conference Report.* London: Family Policy Studies Centre.

Junger-Tas, J. and Terlouw, C. J. (1991) 'Het Nederlands publiek en het criminaliteitsprobleem.' *Delikt en Delinkwent*, March 1991, April 1991.

Kagitcibasi, C. (1996) *Family and Human Development Across Cultures: A View From the Other Side.* Mahwah, New Jersey: Lawrence Erlbaum Associates.

Larzelere, R. and Patterson, G. (1990) 'Parental Management: mediator of the effect of socio-economic status on early delinquency'. *Criminology 28*, 2, 301–324.

Laub, J. and Sampson, R. (1988) 'Unravelling families and delinquency: a re-analysis of the Gluecks' data.' *Criminology 26*, 3, 355–380.

Leach, P. (1999) *The Physical Punishment of Children: Some Input from Recent Research.* London: NSPCC.

Loeber, R., Keenan, K. and Zhang, Q. (1997) 'Boys' experimentation and persistence in developmental pathways towards serious delinquency.' *Journal of Child and Family Studies 6*, 321–357.

Loeber, R. and Stouthamer-Loeber, M. (1986) 'Family factors as correlates and predictors of juvenile conduct problems and delinquency.' In M. Morris and M. Tony (eds) *Crime and Justice 7.* Chicago: University of Chicago Press.

Maccoby, E. and Martin, J. (1983) 'Socialisation in the context of the family: Parent–child interaction.' In E. Hetherington (ed) *Handboook of Child Psychology. Vol.4: Socialisation, Personality, and Social Development.* New York: Wiley.

McCord, J. (1979) 'Some child rearing antecedents of criminal behaviour in adult men.' *Journal of Personality and Social Psychology 37*, 1477–1486.

McCord, J. (1982) 'A longitudinal view of the relationship between parental absence and crime.' In J. Gunn and D. Farrington (eds) *Abnormal Offenders, Delinquency and the Criminal Justice System.* Chichester: Wiley.

Mednick, S., Gabrielli, W. and Hutchings, B. (1984) 'Genetic influences in criminal convictions: evidence from an adoption cohort.' *Science 224*, 891–894.

Moffit, T. E., Caspi, A., Dickson, N., Silva, P. and Stanton, W. (1996) 'Childhood-onset versus adolescent-onset antisocial conduct problems in males: Natural history from ages 3 to 18 years.' *Development and Psychopathology 9*, 399–424.

Osborn, A., Butler, N. and Morris, A. (1984) *The Social Life of Britain's Five-Year-Olds.* London: Routledge and Kegan Paul.

Paikoff, R. L. and Brooks-Gunn, J. (1991) 'Do parent–child relationships change during puberty?' *Psychological Bulletin 110*, 1, 47–66. American Psychological Association, Inc.

Patterson, G. (1980) 'Children who steal.' In T. Hirschi and M. Gottfredson (eds) *Understanding Crime.* Beverly Hills, California: Sage.

Patterson, G. R. (1982) *A Social Learning Approach. Vol. 3: Coercive Family Process.* Eugene, Oregon: Castalia Publishing Co.

Patterson, G. R. (1994) 'Some alternatives to seven myths about treating families of antisocial children.' In C. Henricson (ed) *Crime and the Family*. Conference report. London: Family Policy Studies Centre.

Patterson, G. R. and Forgatch, M. (1987) *Parents and Adolescents Living Together*. Eugene, Oregon: Castalia Publishing Co.

Patterson, G. R. and Narrett, C. M. (1990) 'The development of a reliable and valid treatment program for aggressive young children.' *International Journal of Mental Health 19*, 3, 19–26.

Paulson, S. E. and Sputa, C. L. (1996) Patterns of parenting during adolescence: Perceptions of adolescents and parents. *Adolescence 31*, 370–381.

Peisner, E. S. (1989) 'To spare or not to spare the rod.' In J. Valsiner (ed) *Child Development in Cultural Context*. Toronto: Hogrefe.

Riley, D. and Shaw, M. (1985) *Parental Supervision and Juvenile Delinquency*. Home Office Research Study 83. London: HMSO.

Robins, L. (1978) 'Sturdy childhood predictors of adult anti-social behaviour: replications from longitudinal studies.' *Psychological Medicine 8*, 611–622.

Rutter, M., Giller, H. and Hagell, A. (1998) *Antisocial Behaviour by Young People*. Cambridge: Cambridge University Press.

Shucksmith, J., Hendry, L. and Glendenning, A. (1995) 'Models of parenting: implications for adolescent well being within different types of family contexts.' *Journal of Adolescence 18*, 253–270.

Shulman, S. and Seiffge-Krenke, I. (1997) *Fathers and Adolescents. Developmental and Clinical Perspectives*. (Adolescence and Society Series.) London: Routledge.

Sinha, D. (ed) (1981) *Socialisation of the Indian Child*. New Delhi: Naurang Rai.

Stattin, H. and Magnusson, D. (1996) 'Anti-social development: a holistic approach.' *Development and Psychopathology 8*, 617–645.

Steinberg, L. (1990) 'Autonomy, conflict and harmony in the family relationship.' In S. Feldman and G. Elliott (eds) *At the Threshold: The Developing Adolescent*. Harvard: Harvard University Press.

Straus, M. and Paschall, M. J. (1998) *Corporal Punishment by Mothers and Child's Cognitive Development: a longitudinal study*. Montreal, Canada: World Congress of Sociology.

Straus, M., Sugarman, D. and Giles-Sims, J. (1997). 'Spanking by parents and subsequent antisocial behaviour of children.' *Archives of Pediatrics and Adolescent Medicine 151*, 761–767.

Thompson, E. (2000) *Short and Long Term Effects of Corporal Punishment on Children: A Meta-analytic Review*. University of Texas.

Trommsdorf, G. (1985) 'Some comparative aspects of socialization in Japan and Germany.' In I. R. Lagunes and Y. H. Poortinga (eds) *From a Different Perspective: Studies of Behaviour Across Cultures*. Lisse: Swets and Zeitlinger.

Utting, D., Bright, J. and Henricson, C. (1993) *Crime and the Family. Improving Child Rearing and Preventing Delinquency*. London: Family Policy Studies Centre.

van Voorhis, P., Chenoweth Garner, C., Cullen, F. and Mathers, R. (1988) 'The impact of family structure and quality on delinquency: a comparative assessment of structural and functional factors.' *Criminology 26*, 2.

Wadsworth, M. (1979) *The Roots of Delinquency*. London: Martin Robertson.

Wagner, B., Cohen, P. and Brook, J. (1996) 'Parent–adolescent relationships: moderators of the effects of stressful life events.' *Journal of Adolescent Research 11*, 347–75.

Walters, G. and White, T. (1989) 'Bad genes or bad research?' *Criminology 27*, 3, 455–485.

Wells, L. and Rankin, J. (1988) 'Direct parental controls and delinquency.' *Criminology 26*, 263–285.

Wells, L. and Rankin, J. (1991) 'Families and delinquency: A meta-analysis of the impact of broken homes.' *Social Problems 38*, 71–93.

West, D. (1982) *Delinquency: Its Roots, Careers and Prospects.* London: Heinemann.

West, D. and Farrington, D. (1973) *Who Becomes Delinquent?* London: Heinemann.

West, D. and Farrington, D. (1977) *The Delinquent Way of Life.* London: Heinemann.

Wilson, H. (1980) 'Parental supervision: a neglected aspect of delinquency.' *British Journal of Criminology 20*, 203–235.

Wilson, H. (1987) 'Parental supervision re-examined.' *British Journal of Criminology 27*, 275–301.

Youmiss, J. and Smollar, J. (1985) *Adolescent Relations with Mothers, Fathers and Friends.* Chicago: University of Chicago Press.

Chapter 5

Working with Parents in the Youth Justice Context

Sarah Lindfield and Janice Cusick

Introduction

A new emphasis has been placed on parents' responsibility for their children's offending and antisocial behaviour. The Crime and Disorder Act 1998 created for the first time a principal aim for the youth justice system: to prevent offending by children and young people. One of the six key objectives established to achieve this aim is to reinforce the responsibilities of parents to contribute to the overall aim of preventing offending (Home Office 1998). One mechanism for doing this is the Parenting Order. A Parenting Order can be imposed (under Section 8 of the Crime and Disorder Act 1998) on a parent or guardian when a young person aged 10–17 years has been convicted of a criminal offence, or is made the subject of an Anti-Social Behaviour order, a Child Safety order or a Sex Offender order. Parenting orders can also be made when a parent or guardian has been prosecuted under the Education Act 1996 for their child's non-school attendance. In all circumstances an order should only be made if it would be desirable in the interests of preventing repetition of a young person's behaviour (Home Office 1998).

A Parenting Order requires parents to attend guidance or counselling sessions for up to three months; additionally, parents may be required to exercise control over their children's behaviour for up to twelve months by, for example, ensuring that they are home by a certain time of night. The guidance and counselling element of the Parenting Order is based on research which has shown that authoritarian and permissive parenting styles are linked to youth offending (Graham and Bowling 1995; Utting, Bright and Henricson 1993). The order is designed to secure the attendance of parents on programmes that will strengthen their ability to parent authoritatively. (For a discussion on the influence of different parenting styles on young people's behaviour see Chapter 4.)

The Parenting and Youth Justice project at the Trust for the Study of Adolescence (TSA) is providing support to 42 parenting projects funded under the Youth Justice Board's Development Fund Intervention Programme. The projects are working with parents/carers of young people who are involved in the youth justice system, considered at risk of being so, or who are exhibiting 'antisocial behaviour'. Parenting programmes will be offered by these projects to parents/carers either on a voluntary basis, or as a requirement of a Parenting Order. The projects are based either within Youth Offending Teams (YOTs), or in partner agencies which accept referrals from YOTs. (Multi-agency Youth Offending Teams were established by the Crime and Disorder Act 1998. Agencies that contribute to YOTs are the police, Probation Service, Health Service, Social Services and the Education Department.) Each of the projects is being evaluated at a local level by independent evaluators, as well as at a national level by the Policy Research Bureau. The 42 parenting projects, ourselves as their 'national supporters', the local evaluators and the Policy Research Bureau as national evaluators, have all been funded by the Youth Justice Board to explore the elements of effective practice in this newly developing provision.

The role of the TSA as national supporters is broad and entails the provision of a wide range of support. We began in October 1999 by contacting each of the projects to construct a directory of provision with contact details and a summary of the work of each of the projects. This was subsequently distributed to all Youth Offending Teams. Operating on a needs-led model of support, we then asked each of the projects to identify their support needs and suggest ways in which we could help to meet them. Since that time we have held training events to address the projects' identified needs, created a regional group structure so that projects can share experience and learn from each other, produced the first edition of a bi-annual Parenting and Youth Justice newsletter and continued to work directly with projects as they develop.

In this chapter we will provide an overview of the work with parents that has been developed to respond to Parenting Orders and to address one of the key objectives of the youth justice system: reinforcing parents' responsibilities. Our work has enabled us to learn about the many practice issues that parenting workers face, and we hope in this chapter to highlight some of the key issues and illustrate the ways in which they are beginning to be addressed. We will focus first on the assessment process and the tools used to identify whether a parenting intervention is relevant to a family's circumstances and, if so, what type of intervention would be helpful. Next, we will describe the different programmes and models that are being offered to parents and outline the core elements contained within them. We will go on to describe the practice issues emerging from the delivery of these programmes, and finally we will review ways in which work with parents can also involve their teenagers to provide an integrated service to families.

Parenting assessment

Youth Offending Teams (YOTs) were established by the Crime and Disorder Act 1998 (CDA), as a multi-agency organisation whose duties include co-ordinating service provision to prevent re-offending and to target the risk factors associated with youth crime. They have been given the co-ordinating role for Parenting Orders, which includes the provision of Responsible Officers to hold the order, and either to work directly with parents themselves or to arrange that someone else does so.

The Responsible Officer role may be held by a member of the YOT or by staff in Social Services Children and Family or Adolescent teams, if they are already involved with a family, or by probation officers. The CDA made no provision for education welfare officers or for education social workers to take on this role. However, the Criminal Justice and Court Services Act 2000 (Part IV, Chapter 1, section 73), implemented in April 2001, amends the CDA to enable local education authority staff to become Responsible Officers when Parenting Orders are made under the Education Act 1996. This may help to avoid bringing families whose children have not committed an offence into the youth justice arena.

As co-ordinators of service provision, YOTs need to carry out an initial assessment to identify whether a parenting intervention is relevant, and if so, what type of programme should be offered (see Figure 5.1 on p.80 for an outline of the assessment process). The practice of assessing need should be interactive, ideally involving the whole family. This is a new departure for some youth justice workers who are more familiar with focusing on young people and relating to their families mainly as a way of facilitating this work. To assist YOT staff in this unfamiliar task, an assessment tool

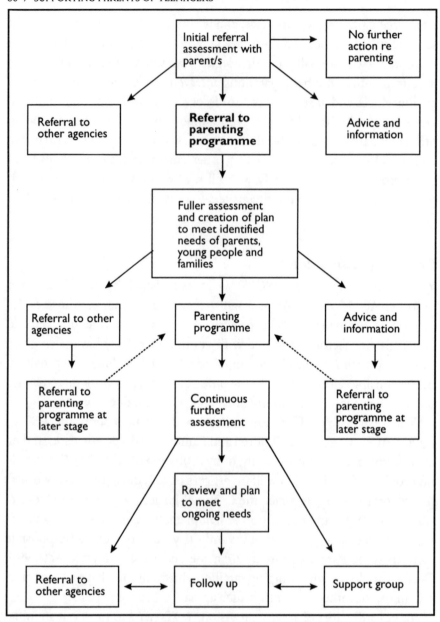

Figure 5.1. Flowchart of the Assessment Process

this work. To assist YOT staff in this unfamiliar task, an assessment tool designed for use in the youth justice context has recently been developed.

The Parenting Assessment Tool for Youth Offending Teams (Henricson, Coleman and Roker 2000) enables youth justice workers to identify whether parenting behaviours that are risk factors for youth offending are present. The following four risk factors have been identified as most amenable to change:

- serious deficiencies with supervision and monitoring
- absence of discipline
- harsh or seriously inconsistent discipline
- absence of communication and support.

(Also identified as risk factors are parental and sibling criminality and neglect or abuse, none of which are appropriately dealt with in this context.)

YOTs are required to assess the needs of young people who are referred to them using the ASSET assessment tool. (The Parenting Assessment Tool has been designed to be used in conjunction with the ASSET form to avoid duplication of assessment.) Information gained from completing the ASSET will contribute to the decision to offer a parenting intervention. Information from other agencies will also supplement the direct assessment process.

The first stage of assessment for YOTs is to build a relationship with young people, their parents and other family members and to work with them to identify whether these risk factors are present. Clarity about the purpose of the assessment and an emphasis on identifying parenting strengths, as well as risk factors and needs, will help parents to feel respected. This task demands a high level of skill, as parents may well be feeling hostile to a process that they see as punishing them for their child's behaviour and which calls into question their parenting skills. They may be feeling anger, guilt, resentment and hopelessness. An additional layer of concern for parents is the knowledge that the outcome of the assessment process may be that a verbal or written report is presented in court and magistrates may decide to make a Parenting Order. Clearly, the worker needs to address this issue during the assessment process and respond to the difficulties that this is likely to cause parents.

During the pilot phase of Parenting Orders, when nine YOTs trialled the new order, many workers took the approach that it would be more appropriate to work with parents on a voluntary rather than a statutory basis. There were two main reason for this: first, that engaging with parents in partnership rather than in a coercive relationship would be more conducive to adult learning; second, and perhaps more important, workers were reluctant to initiate proceedings which might lead to criminal sanctions if parents did not comply with the requirements of an order, which ultimately could lead to a custodial sentence. (Breach of a Parenting Order cannot directly result in a custodial sentence for parents. However, it can result in a community sentence or a fine being imposed, and non-payment of fines is an imprisonable offence.) For some parenting workers involved in the pilot phase there seems to have been a shift in thinking about this issue. They reported that in some situations parents would agree that a parenting intervention was relevant and agree to take part voluntarily in a programme, but did not subsequently do so. Other parents, on being issued Parenting Orders, reported that they had been angry about having to attend a programme and would not have done so without an order being in force, but that they had found the programme very useful. These experiences caused some parenting workers to reconsider their approach to the value of Parenting Orders. However, this issue is still under debate and we do not yet have research findings which can identify the impacts of voluntary or statutory provision, nor the effectiveness of the interventions currently offered to parents. Only practical experience linked to research findings will help to identify their effectiveness in ensuring that parents attend programmes designed to strengthen their parenting.

The recent introduction of the Human Rights Act 1998 has added to concerns about the use of Parenting Orders. In the view of some legal advisers to magistrates, Parenting Orders may not be compatible with the rights stated in articles 6, 7 and 8 – the right to a fair trial, no punishment without law, and the right to respect for private and family life. It is likely that at some point in the near future there will be a challenge to Parenting Orders under the Human Rights Act and this will help to establish their legitimacy. Meanwhile, YOTs are working with parents, within the context of the approach of their local magistrates, to assess parents positively and to provide the most appropriate services, whether through voluntary agreement or a Parenting Order.

An important part of the assessment process is to explore with parents any significant stresses that they may be experiencing which place a strain on their parenting and on the family as a whole. These may include poverty, racism, inadequate accommodation, disability, and so on. Staff need to be realistic with parents about what can be covered in a parenting intervention, but the more intensive and systemic interventions will help parents to address these types of issues. (See the section 'More practice issues' below for a discussion about the length and intensity of programmes. An example of a family-based parenting intervention which addresses stress factors in all areas of family life is multisystemic therapy, which has been found to be successful in reducing problem behaviours and improving family relationships (Henggeler, Melton and Smith 1992).) Sometimes specialist help will be preferable to a referral to a locally available parenting programme. It may be more appropriate for issues such as, for example, bereavement, parental alcohol or other drug abuse, mental and physical health needs and high levels of family conflict to be dealt with by a specialist agency. Identifying these issues and taking appropriate action is an element of assessment of need that should be continuous during the delivery of any intervention. In addition, it is helpful to monitor gaps in the services provided to meet parents' identified needs. This information can then be compiled and used to lobby local and national government and other funding providers to establish the provision of necessary services.

If YOT staff and magistrates have a good understanding of parenting risk factors this will help to ensure that Parenting Orders and referrals to parenting programmes are only made when an assessment has identified that the risk factors are present. Well-constructed gate-keeping procedures within YOTs will also ensure that they are not made when factors other than parenting style are contributing to a young person's offending behaviour.

When carrying out assessments consideration needs to be given to cultural differences in parenting and to the realities and needs of different ethnic groups. Cultural awareness training for staff may help to ensure that assessments take account of the differences as well as the similarities between parenting practices in different cultures. The use of interpreters may be necessary so that parents with English as a second language have the opportunity to engage fully in the assessment process.

The full range of family structures needs to be encompassed so that members of the extended family, for example, step-parents and absent fathers, who are involved in a young person's life, are also involved in the assessment process. If there are two parents involved, then both should be given the opportunity to take part. The issue of domestic abuse, clearly, may need to be addressed. We discuss this in the 'more practice issues' section.

There are a number of assessment tools for measuring behavioural difficulties in the young person, parental self-esteem, and family functioning. (The Strengths and Difficulties Questionnaire, developed by Robert Goodman, and the Family Grid, by Hilton Davies, are two assessment tools developed for use in the wider parenting field and which encompass the teenage years.) These can provide additional information to identify the functionality or dysfunctionality of family processes, and therefore help to indicate the type of programme which may be helpful for parents and families. These assessment tools can also contribute data to a programme evaluation if used before and after an intervention: the differences between the two sets of information can be compared to see what benefits there have been for the parent/s. This data can be supplemented with an equivalent process for young people and others, such as teachers, who are in a position to observe changes in behaviour and attitudes. A parallel assessment tool completed by a young person not only contributes to the measurement of effectiveness of the intervention, it can also help to highlight the issues to be addressed when involving young people in the parenting intervention (see section 'Involving young children' below).

When all available information has been gathered, assessors will need to work with parents to decide an appropriate course of action. This may entail a referral to a parenting programme, in which case the most appropriate intervention will need to be selected, based on the broad range of information gathered in the assessment process. Any referral should consider what types of programmes are available within the locality and any problems parents would have in accessing them. Childcare, transport and finance relating to these issues need to be addressed before offering any intervention.

Summary

The assessment processes of YOTs appear to vary greatly. Some employ what might be described as an 'intuitive' approach to deciding whether support services should be offered to parents, and if so, what these services should be. Other YOTs have developed a structured assessment format that identifies risk and protective factors within families and takes into account the different family circumstances which will influence how appropriate services can be made available to them. The TSA intends to work with practitioners to establish quality standards for this crucial assessment phase so that practice is consistent and reliable, and to ensure that the needs of parents and families in all their complexity are recognised and addressed.

As we have highlighted in this section, the assessment process is the key to the delivery of relevant and helpful services to parents and families. Once you have started to identify parenting strengths, you can establish which services can be offered to build on those strengths and to address gaps or weaknesses. You will also have begun to establish a relationship that can help parents to feel respected, listened to and understood. These are the foundations on which an effective service can be built.

In the next section we describe some of the programmes devised by Youth Offending Teams and their partner agencies to address the support needs of parents identified in the assessment process.

Programmes to support parents

The implementation of the Crime and Disorder Act 1998 has caused a rapid expansion in the number of projects providing support to parents of teenagers involved in the youth justice system, or who are considered to be 'at risk' of offending. There are a variety of parenting interventions that have been developed to support parents in this context (see Figure 2 below). We have selected some to discuss in detail here which have either been adapted from existing programmes aimed at parents of younger children, or which have been specifically developed to support this group of families. They should help to illustrate the different ways in which YOTs (alongside their partner agencies) are responding to the statutory requirement that they co-ordinate the provision of services to parents while developing a more integrated and preventative approach to youth offending which addresses the full range of identified risk factors. The parenting interventions listed in Figure 2 are described in more detail in *Working with Parents in the Youth Justice Context* (Cusick, Lindfield and Coleman 2000).

Individual family-based programmes:
PARENTING ADOLESCENTS WISELY

This is a CD-ROM-based multimedia programme which parents can use by themselves to explore different parenting scenarios and to develop helpful skills and strategies. The original USA version is being used by some YOTs, while a UK version is being developed by the Greater Manchester Crime and Disorder Partnership with Prof. Don Gordon, who designed the original programme. The Manchester project will offer the programme in three ways:

- as an individual parent/carer intervention only
- providing sessions with a consultant in addition to individual use of the programme

- **Individual/couple therapy** of different types that can be offered when parents' needs must be addressed before they can focus on parenting issues.

- **Individual/couple cognitive behaviour multimedia programmes**, such as 'Parenting Adolescents Wisely' and the Parent/Child videotape modelling series (Webster Stratton), designed for parents of younger children. These programmes can be used with or without therapeutic input and also in group settings.

- **Mentoring**: linking of a parent/carer with a volunteer mentor who can provide guidance and support the development of skills and knowledge.

- **Parent adviser**: an adviser builds a relationship with the parent/s and offers counselling and guidance in the home. An approach that can combine both individual and group activities as an initial, individual intervention might lead on in some cases to group-based activity.

- **Individual family-based therapy**, e.g. standard parent/carer and child therapy offered by Child and Adolescent Mental Health services.

- **Multisystemic therapy** is an intensive therapeutic approach, which can be home- or community-based, and which addresses issues in the interconnected systems of family, school, peer, and welfare.

- **Functional family therapy**, involving the whole family to improve communication and levels of support between family members.

- **Solution-focused (brief) therapy**: a short-term intervention assisting participants to explore future solutions rather than past problems.

- **Family group conferencing**: the whole family is involved in creating a plan for change.

- **Group-based programmes** focused on parents/carers of young people who have offended.

- **Group-based programmes** designed for a wider client group of parents/carers of young people considered at risk of offending or who are behaving 'anti-socially'.

- **Group-based programmes** delivered on a universal basis and designed for any parent/carer of a pre-teen or teenager.

(Cusick, Lindfield and Coleman 2000)

Figure 5.2. Models of Parenting Interventions

- using the programme in a group setting.

It is a cognitive behavioural programme that is interactive and does not require any previous computing skills, as the process is simple.

SOLUTION-FOCUSED BRIEF THERAPY

North Devon YOT is using a family therapy model that draws on solution-focused brief therapy (SFBT) techniques, Bowen's natural systems theory, and restorative and positive conflict resolution practices.

A number of other YOTs have been trained in SFBT, as its 'here and now' problem-solving approach can be useful when working with a variety of client groups. Mutale (2000) stresses its value as a more culturally responsive way of working with families so as to acknowledge the 'importance of each family's strengths and [to] use the family's metaphors to construct a more empowering and pro-social approach to life' (p.3). He also suggests that the SFBT emphasis on functionality rather than dysfunctionality can help to redress past negative contact with professionals, which may have been experienced by minority ethnic groups and families of young people who are offending.

TELEPHONE HELPLINE AND TELEPHONE SUPPORT

Parentline Plus offers a freephone helpline service for parents in distress, providing information about parenting issues and organisations available to provide further assistance in relation to family change, divorce, separation and specific issues, such as young people's drug misuse, educational problems and criminal activity. The training of helpline staff has been extended to include issues commonly faced by parents of adolescents and where their teenager is having difficulty at school or is involved in the Youth Justice System.

A telephone support service is also being piloted by Parentline Plus in partnership with Essex Social Services (Basildon) and Wirral Youth Offending Team. Parents referred to the service will receive weekly pre-arranged telephone calls from trained supporters for 6 to 8 weeks. The supporters will help parents to identify difficulties, discuss them and agree steps to make changes. Each week progress will be discussed, and new goals set as progress is made and changes are achieved. Parentline Plus aims to develop this service more widely in 2001.

Group-based programmes:

'LET'S TALK PARENTING'

'Let's Talk Parenting' was commissioned by Northumbria Probation Service and developed by Sue Miller and Joe Ward from the 'Positive Parenting' programme (initially designed for the parents of young children) into a new course for parents of children and young people of all ages. It was piloted by Sunderland YOT, and a number of other YOTs have since received training to deliver the programme to parents.

The new 'Let's Talk Parenting' embodies the same theoretical approach as 'Positive Parenting', with modifications designed to make the course materials easier to assimilate, and to alter the skills content so as to address the needs of parents of older, adolescent children. The eight-session course covers: getting to know each other; the parenting job; naming feelings; getting along together; understanding each other; making choices; setting an example; where do we go from here? Before focusing on problems, the initial session is designed to develop parents' self-awareness and confidence through consideration of their thoughts about childhood and positive feelings towards their children. Information enabling the course facilitators to meet the individual requirements of group participants is gathered prior to the course, and also emerges during the development of individual action plans within the group.

'LIVING WITH TEENAGERS' – CENTRE FOR FUN AND FAMILIES

The Centre for Fun and Families has been running 'Living with Teenagers' groups for parents of teenage children for six years. The programme was developed from their 'Fun and Families' groups for parents with young children.

The centre receives referrals from the local YOTs and other agencies and, perhaps uniquely at this time, they accept self-referrals from parents directly to the centre. Parents may therefore be on an order, or attending voluntarily. Staff have trained a number of YOTs to facilitate 'Living with Teenagers' group programmes.

'Living with Teenagers' is a seven-week parent training programme designed to help parents whose young people are displaying a range of behaviour difficulties such as aggression, defiance, school refusal, bad language, staying out late, stealing, drug or alcohol abuse. The main objective of the group is to apply social learning theory or behavioural principles to individual family circumstances. It is designed to help parents make sense of what their teenagers are doing and why. It is intended to give practical, down-to-earth suggestions to assist them in changing their teenagers' behaviour, and to allow them to recover parenthood as a positive or 'fun' experience. The objective of the groups is to reduce family conflict, improve parents' listening, communication, negotiating and problem-solving skills, and assist parents in setting realistic boundaries.

The centre also run parallel six-week groups called 'Avoiding Conflict with Adults', designed for the teenagers of parents attending the 'Living with Teenagers' groups. This young people's group programme is described in more detail in the section on 'Involving young people'.

[Information reproduced with permission from the Centre for Fun and Families April 2000]

'LIVING WITH TEENAGERS' – RELATE

Relate has recently developed a group programme for parents also called 'Living with Teenagers'. After the initial pilot phase working with Somerset YOT, Relate has now been contracted by other YOTs to provide this course. The programme is held over eight weeks and helps parents share their perceptions of parenting. Group members have the opportunity to reflect on their experiences of being parented and identify the impacts this has had on their own parenting style. The programme is delivered by Relate trained group facilitators. It is accredited through the Open College Network so that parents can receive credits for participating on the course, which they can use in other adult education settings. Referrals are received from Youth Offending Teams, schools and child and family teams within social services departments.

'STRENGTHENING FAMILIES, STRENGTHENING COMMUNITIES'

The Race Equality Unit (REU), with the support of Dr Marilyn Steele, an American child psychologist, is developing an American programme, 'Strengthening Families, Strengthening Communities', so that it can be delivered effectively to families in the UK, especially to Britain's black and minority ethnic communities. The programme is designed for parents of children and young people aged 3–18. It is currently being piloted for parents of young people who have offended, or are considered at risk of offending, at the Holloway Neighbourhood Group and at the Dalston Youth Project.

The programme uses a strengths-based 'facilitative model' which aims to raise the consciousness of parents. In addition, the curriculum aims to help families develop:

- strong ethnic and cultural roots
- positive parent–child relationships
- a range of life skills
- self-esteem, self-discipline and social competence
- ability to access community resources.

The aims of the programme are achieved through a range of methods, which include:

- providing parents with information to empower them
- developing anger management and positive discipline techniques
- providing a cultural framework to validate the historical and family experiences of different ethnic groups
- decreasing isolation by helping parents to connect to community resources.

The programme is structured into 12 three-hour sessions (plus an orientation session) taught in consecutive weeks. It is run with groups of 8–20 parents. To facilitate attendance, transport is provided, as are childcare and refreshments.

The REU is working to achieve accreditation for the programme through the Open College Network that will enable parents to develop a portfolio and gain a qualification for participating in the programme.

[Information reproduced with permission from REU January 2000]

'SURVIVING ADOLESCENCE'

Parentline Plus has developed a new group programme from their two core programmes, 'Being a Parent' and 'Parenting Matters'. 'Surviving Adolescence' is for parents of adolescents, particularly those who have a high level of need and are struggling to deal with their teenagers' difficult behaviours. The programme runs for eight sessions and is delivered by trained Parentline Plus facilitators who receive referrals from Youth Offending Teams. The aims of the programme are to:

- help give parents/carers an opportunity to reflect on their role, and to feel supported

- enhance participants' communication and problem-solving skills

- help participants to deal with difficult behaviour and understand the needs of teenagers.

The programme is designed for parents who attend voluntarily as well as parents on court orders, and is used by Gloucester, Harrow and West Sussex YOTs.

'TEENAGERS IN TROUBLE – SKILLS FOR PARENTS'

A video has been produced by the TSA, with funding from the Youth Justice Board, specifically for work with parents whose teenagers are offending. It can be used flexibly, either in groups or with individual parents. Three families are portrayed by actors in scenarios that are used to highlight common problems and experiences. Topics include:

- how parent's feelings affect the way they relate to their teenager

- communication issues – strategies and skills for positive communication

- boundaries – negotiating what is acceptable and recognising what can be of use

- negotiating – and the relevance of this in getting on with teenagers

- parent disagreement – shares points about avoiding major disagreements and rows in front of teenagers

- neighbourhood and peer influences and how these issues can impact on teenage behaviour.

Each scenario is followed by a discussion involving parents, most of whom have previously taken part in a parenting programme to help them resolve difficulties with their teenagers. The video is accompanied by a guide for parents and a guide for facilitators, expanding on the issues raised in the video and including key learning points and homework suggestions. The video was designed to fill a gap in the materials available for parenting programmes, as it portrays the more difficult to handle situations and relationships which families can experience.

Several YOTs are incorporating sections of the video in their group programmes, and Oxford Parent Education Team in partnership with Oxford YOT has developed a group programme based on the structure of the video.

YOUTH OFFENDING TEAM GROUP PROGRAMMES

Many of the new parenting programme staff in, or attached to, YOTs have reported that they are involved in a process that could be described as 'cherry-picking'. Rather than using existing complete packages, they are choosing to adapt materials from a number of parenting programmes that have been designed for work with parents of teenagers or younger children, and to construct new programmes for work with parents of teenagers in difficulty. This has helped them to construct programmes that they see as more relevant to the group of parents they are working with, and to their style of group facilitation. When they have been tested and grounded in practice, the newly developed programmes should provide a wealth of materials to be drawn on and, if tightly evaluated, will provide valuable information of what works in this field.

The Family Caring Trust (FCT) 'Parenting Teenagers' programme materials have in some areas provided the foundation for YOT programmes. The FCT materials are a series of flexible, easy-to-run self-help programmes for the parents of teenagers. There are instructions for each session, and audio and video tapes depicting family scenarios. The programmes are broad-based, drawing on family systems, humanistic, Adlerian and social learning approaches. Outcomes for parents have included improved listening, communication and discipline skills and the adoption of new approaches to parenting, with children acquiring a greater sense of responsibility and engaging in more pro-social behaviour (Smith 1996).

By comparing a number of different group programmes currently being used by YOTs and their partner agencies, it is possible to identify common topic areas that can be described as core elements. These are included in parenting programmes in order to address the risk and protective factors and to break the links between parenting and youth offending or antisocial behaviour.

Core elements of programmes

With growing understanding of the links between parenting and youth offending or antisocial behaviour (see above), parenting programmes are increasingly able to focus on strengthening identified family protective factors and reducing risk factors.

- Supportive parent–child relationships
- Positive discipline methods
- Monitoring and supervision
- Families who advocate for their children
- Parents who seek information and support

(Kumpfer and Alvarado 1998 p.3)

Figure 5.3. Family Protective Factors

Parenting programmes that describe themselves as strengths-based are more likely to be able to move from rhetoric to reality if they carry out a thorough assessment process, as we have outlined above. This will enable them to identify strengths that can be enhanced for effective parenting, as well as the situational and personal parent and youth risk characteristics (Brown 1998). Situational risk characteristics include poverty, a high degree of conflict between parents, and neighbourhood violence. Personal parent risk factors include being recipients of inadequate parenting themselves, having mental health issues, and being drug- or alcohol-addicted (Brown 1998). Risk factors for young people include low attachment to family and school and high attachment to delinquent peers. Research studies in the USA suggest that 'parenting and family interventions that decrease family conflict and improve family involvement and parental monitoring should reduce problem behaviours' (Kumpfer and Alvarado 1998 p.2).

Individual and family-based parenting programmes can more easily be designed to address the specific protective and risk factors identified in the assessment process. However, flexibly designed group programmes are also able to focus on the issues most relevant to the group's members and can be structured to build on parenting strengths.

The core elements can be categorised, like a job specification for parenting, under the following headings:

KNOWLEDGE

adolescent behaviour – child development
parenting styles – authoritarian, permissive, authoritative
cultural background – influence on parenting role
resources – accessing all sorts of support: friends, specialist agencies, etc.

SKILLS

communication – active listening, etc.
conflict resolution – assertiveness, negotiation, etc.
setting boundaries – 'I' statements, behaviour charts, etc.
problem-solving – family meetings, generating options, etc.

ATTITUDES

discipline methods – alternatives to use of physical punishment
being a parent – responsibilities and rights and social context
being a teenager – responsibilities and rights and social context
potential for change – belief and indicators that change is possible

EXPERIENCE

own adolescence – how past impacts on present, and connecting up
sharing own experience of what works – who, when, where, how and why

These core elements may be supplemented with additional topics relevant to group members, such as alcohol and other drug misuse, step-parenting issues, divorce and separation, and so on. Some of the core elements could be categorised under a number of headings. Discipline, for example, could be discussed in terms of *attitudes*, which could be linked to own *experience* of punishment as a child, which could be followed by practising *skills*, which can be used to support *knowledge* of other discipline methods.

Programmes such as Parenting Wisely (CD-ROM) and the 'Teenagers in Trouble' video that can be used with individuals or families as well as groups, incorporate these core elements too. They also emphasise the need for skills to be practised by parents, which is an integral part of the group programme structure. 'Information alone has not been found to have an impact on behaviour unless combined with discussion time, experiential practice, role-playing and homework to solidify behavioural changes'

(Kumpfer 1998 p.6). Varying learning methods also helps to reflect the diversity of participants' learning styles and experiences.

More practice issues

It is crucial that the core elements, as well as the programme structure, acknowledge and reflect the diversity of experience of participants in the programme. This is likely to include diversity of culture and ethnicity, of socio-economic status, levels of education, literacy, family structure, language, disability and sexuality, among the full range of human diversity.

Literacy

The variation in levels of literacy among group members has emerged as an issue for many facilitators, who are finding that they need to be creative about the ways in which they record and display information to make it accessible to the whole group. Using video and audio material, discussion time and role play are all ways of making programme content accessible to people with low levels of literacy. Graphics that represent emotions, ideas and concepts can be used in place of words when facilitating exercises such as creating a behaviour chart or setting boundaries. Some projects are moving forward on developing these materials for groups. The Centre for Fun and Families, for example, has devised symbols to represent time intervals that can be used when illustrating the use of charts. A picture of 'Coronation Street', which is on TV on alternate days, is used to represent something that happens every other day. 'Emmerdale' could be used for every weekday, and times can be linked to other well-known TV programmes, so that 'be in by 10 o'clock' could be illustrated by a picture of a nightly news programme. As was pointed out in a recent discussion which involved Parents for Prevention (Birmingham) and the Centre for Fun and Families (Leicester), care needs to be taken to ensure that the symbols used are culturally relevant to the group's participants. This discussion took place at the Midlands regional group meeting for Youth Justice Board funded parenting projects. Regional group meetings are also being held by YOTs not receiving YJB funding and the two structures may combine in the near future as TSA has recently been funded to provide support on a regional basis to all YOTs.

Culture and ethnicity

Addressing the needs of parents from different cultures and of different ethnicity is a vital part of providing effective services. Parenting workers have reported a number of ways in which they have developed their practice to work with a family from a different culture or ethnicity than their own:

- acknowledging and being open about the differences
- liaising with a relevant community group to learn more about the culture
- recruiting a cultural adviser with knowledge of a particular culture or ethnic group
- co-working with a worker from the same cultural background and ethnicity as the parent/s
- listening to the parents' description of their cultural norms, particularly in relation to parenting
- working with the extended family and community elders, if helpful to the family
- working with individual families rather than referring them to a group
- running a group for members of a specific community or ethnic group.

Spending time to learn what is needed before and during an intervention is clearly necessary, as is the allocation of other resources that will facilitate the provision of culturally relevant services, such as employing appropriate interpreters and translating programme materials. Group workers need to consider how their programme will reflect participants' different cultural backgrounds and ethnicity in the way that the programme is structured, in its content and in the materials used. It may also be helpful to provide culturally or ethnically specific groups to engage parents. Establishing links with different community groups and services may help to extend the range of programmes which can be provided for different groups within a locality.

Gender

TSA sent out a questionnaire to all YOTs to find out about their work with parents. This included a question on the gender of parents made subject to a Parenting Order. The results are currently being analysed but our impression is that orders are mainly being made on mothers, whether or not they are single parents. It appears that this may be because more women than men attend court and magistrates prefer to make orders when those receiving them are present in court, being reluctant to delay the court process until both parents are present, since any delay would conflict with the aim of speeding up youth justice. This raises equality issues for both women and men, as women are given total responsibility for their children's behaviour, and men are not being recognised as responsible fathers. 'There is evidence to suggest that parenting programmes which only involve one parent can disrupt family life and have a detrimental effect on marital relations' (Henricson 1998 p.11). In some areas there has been a challenge to the making of orders on women alone, and magistrates are ensuring that where there is, or may be, positive involvement of a father in a young person's life, he is also being made subject to the order. Fathers may be required to attend court when the making of an order is anticipated, an order may be made in their absence or they may be invited to attend a voluntary programme. (The court, before making an order, has to explain to the parent/s 'in ordinary language' the requirements of the order, the consequences of failure to comply with it and the right to request a review of the order (Section 9 (3) Crime and Disorder Act 1998). Some courts have taken the approach that they can fulfil this requirement, when they anticipate making an order, by sending a letter and then making an order in the absence of the parent/s if they do not attend the next court date.)

Domestic abuse

When conflict between parents is high, then the option of providing separate but complementary services needs to be considered. It may be appropriate to refer a couple to a counselling service such as Relate, to family mediation or to family therapy. Individual work with each parent could be considered, either before or alongside participation in a group programme. Screening for domestic abuse and providing services when it is present, is an area that requires further development. The more YOTs engage with families, the more likely they are to identify issues of abuse, including the abuse of children, which will require them to take action to ensure the safety of all concerned. The earlier abuse can be identified, the more possible it is to provide services that are relevant to each family's situation. The assessment process offers an opportunity to address issues of violence within the family and to determine the appropriate course of action. It may be relevant to adopt practices used in family mediation, where couples are met with separately, so that issues of violence within the family can emerge in confidence. One project has offered separate provision for a couple where conflict was high. They each attended a group running at the same time but in different parts of the city. Another project has offered men- and women-only groups, as they found that in their first groups women were disclosing both that they were experiencing domestic abuse and that they had been sexually abused as children. Group facilitators need to build into their programmes and co-working structures a plan for responding to such disclosures, which reflects the needs of those involved and helps to ensure their safety, as well as addressing the other group participants' interests.

Child protection

Positive discipline is one of the core elements in parenting programmes, as the way parents discipline their children is a key risk or protective factor in relation to youth offending, antisocial behaviour and violent behaviour later in life (Lyon 2000). Addressing this topic may entail a discussion about the discipline methods used currently by parents. Again, workers need to be clear about how they will respond to any indication that a young person is being harmed by parental discipline. A good knowledge of child protection procedures and discussion with the Area Child Protection Committee about programme content, what might emerge during the programme and how it should be dealt with, will help to ensure that workers are more confident about responding to child protection concerns. Being clear about the limits of confidentiality without closing down discussion is obviously a balancing act that all family workers face. Parenting workers, however, have the opportunity to address discipline methods directly and to offer alternative strategies, skills, practice time and support to help parents develop different approaches to discipline.

Length and intensity of programmes

The Parenting Order legislation does not stipulate the number of sessions to be included in the three-month guidance and counselling requirement of the order. However, it does stipulate that the sessions should be no more than weekly, and should run concurrently. This suggests that the maximum number of sessions possible in this requirement of the order would be twelve. However, if a group programme was recommended post assessment, the likelihood of there being a group starting the week the order is made is slim, given that most YOTs and partner agencies are using a closed group model rather than an open, rolling programme. Providers will need to give some thought to arrangements that can be made to provide support for parents before they embark on the programme, and to sustain their motivation and commitment while they are waiting for a group to start. Two approaches to this issue have emerged recently. First, a drop-in facility can be established for parents who are on a group programme waiting list. This enables parents to gain support from each other and from staff in an informal setting. Second, information sessions are provided covering topics such as substance misuse, the youth justice system, and so on. These could again be informal and based on the assessment of need previously undertaken.

The length and intensity of programmes, and therefore the number of core elements that are included, varies greatly from six weekly, one-hour sessions in one YOT to the twelve weekly, three-hour sessions of the Race Equality Unit's 'Strengthening Families, Strengthening Communities' programme.

For high-risk families facing more complex difficulties and with highly dysfunctional processes, it has been estimated that interventions need to last between 30 and 45 hours in order to have a positive and lasting impact. 'Many parent education or training interventions fail with high risk families because they are too short to really reduce risk-producing processes and behaviours and increase protective processes and behaviours in these parents' (Kumpfer and Alvarado 1998, p.8). It is also suggested that programmes that do not incorporate enough time to practise each skill taught are less effective in changing behaviours (Kumpfer and Alvarado 1998).

As the number of parents who have participated in specialist programmes is increasing, YOTs and their partner agencies are beginning to explore how they can provide support after a programme has been completed, in order to maximise effectiveness. Follow-up group or individual sessions at three- and six-monthly intervals, parent-led support groups, drop-in centres and telephone contact are all being considered by programme providers to assist parents at the stage where they are integrating new learning into everyday life.

A review of parenting programmes in the USA that have been given 'exemplary' status under the Office of Juvenile Justice and Delinquency Program's 'Strengthening America's Families' initiative to identify effective programmes, reveals a similar range of length and intensity to UK group programmes (see Table 5.1). Practice in the UK may be influenced pragmatically by the length of Parenting Orders and by the availability of resources. Programme providers are also likely to be balancing the inclusion of core elements to address identified needs, with an attempt to ensure that families are not alienated by the time commitment required for a lengthy programme, or one consisting of lengthy sessions at an inconvenient time of day.

The Parenting Order legislation stipulates that programmes should attempt to avoid conflict with a parent's religious beliefs and not interfere with their work or education (Section 9 (4) Crime and Disorder Act 1998). A range of other factors that may affect parents' ability and commitment to participating in the programme will also need to be considered. As we mentioned above, the assessment process is key to establishing the most appropriate way to structure a programme, and workers at this stage can begin to make arrangements to address the issues which affect individual parents. Some projects have been able to secure funding to provide childcare, transport and refreshments (which can range from providing tea, coffee and biscuits at each session, to funding a take-away dinner on the final session of a group programme).

Local social services' policies and the legal framework for childcare have caused difficulties for some YOTs as they are unable to provide funding for childcare unless it is provided by a registered childminder or nursery. One response to this may be that parents are offered a sum of money for unspecified expenses, enabling them to make their own arrangements so as to be able to attend a parenting programme. The provision of a crèche on site could be a positive alternative to this dilemma.

Many YOTs are working with parents individually, either when there are not enough people for a group in their area, or if the assessment has shown the need for an individual programme. There is very little information about structured individual work with parents and its effectiveness, other than the 'Parenting Adolescents Wisely' CD-ROM programme, and this does not require the presence of a parenting worker. This programme (described above) may be offered for parents to use for one or two sessions only, and yet has been shown to be effective in increasing the use of parenting skills taught in the programme and in reducing young people's

Table 5.1 'Exemplary' programmes in the USA (from Kumpfer 1993, Strengthening America's Families)

Title	Description	Type	Goal	Aimed at	Duration	Follow-up
'Strengthening Families' programme	Family skills training 10–14 years	Printed material and videos	Reduce substance use and behaviour problems	Parents and youth	7 x 2 hr sessions	Four sessions six months to one year after initial sessions
'Adolescent Transitions' programme	Parent training 11–18 years	12 parent group meetings and 4 individual family meetings, 6 videos, and mid-week phone contact	Stop development of teen antisocial behaviours and drug experimentation	Parents	Group meeting lasting 90 minutes once a week	Monthly sessions for at least three months
Brief strategic family therapy	Family therapy 8–17 years	Therapists working with the family	Prevent and treat child and adolescent behaviour problems and mild substance abuse	Family	12–15 sessions of 60–90 min. over 3 months	
Multidimensional family therapy	Family therapy 11–18 years	Therapists working with the family	Deal with drug and behaviour problems	Family	16–25 sessions over 4 to 6 months	
'Parenting Wisely'	Parent training 6–18 years	Interactive CD-ROM	Reduce delinquency, substance abuse and involvement with juvenile justice system	Family	1–2 x 3 hr sessions	
Treatment foster care	Parent training 12–18 years	6 months placement with foster parents for 12–18-year-olds	Reduce criminal behaviour and substance use and improve school attendance	Parents and youth	6 months placement with daily behaviour management progr. for the youth and weekly therapy sessions for both youth and parents	12 months aftercare
'Strengthening Families' programme	Family skills training 6–10 years		Reduce risk factors for substance use and other problem behaviours of high-risk children of substance abusers (also used for non-substance abusing parents)	Family	14 x 2 hr meetings weekly	
'Preparing for the Drug-Free Years'	Parent training 8–14 years	Workshops	Reduce adolescent drug abuse and behaviour problems	Parents	5 x 2 hr sessions or 10 x 1 hr sessions	
Multisystemic therapy programme	Comprehensive 10–18		Reduce antisocial behaviour in adolescents	Family	2–15 hrs weekly for four to six months	Aftercare
Functional family therapy	Family therapy 6–18 years	Therapists working with the family	Help families with acting-out youth	Family		

problem behaviours (Gordon and Kacir 1997, in Coleman, Henricson and Roker 1999).

Although the content, length and intensity of parenting programmes are important, so too are the skills of the facilitator, therapist or parent supporter. These roles demand a high level of skill to build relationships that support parents' development of skills and confidence in their parenting, in often very difficult and stressful situations.

Summary

Clearly, evaluation findings from the 42 Intervention Programme projects, as well as from other YOTs and their partner agencies, will help to identify the effectiveness of some of the broader aspects of the newly developing parenting programmes. As this field develops, more research projects looking at the detail of the ingredients of effective programmes will help us to set quality standards for the UK. It will be helpful to know more, for example, about the core skills required of programme staff, the optimal length and intensity of programmes, the effectiveness of mixed groups or groups aimed at a particular community of interest – for example, groups specifically for fathers, black parents or parents of persistently offending young people – and whether voluntary or compulsory interventions show the same levels of effectiveness. Another ingredient that many projects are now beginning to address is how best to involve young people in parenting interventions. In the next section we will explore current practice in the UK and highlight some successful approaches that are being used in the USA.

Involving young people

Research into the effectiveness of family interventions in the USA has shown that 'family-focussed programmes are more effective than programmes that focus solely on the child or the parents' (Kumpfer and Alvarado 1998 p.7). Given these findings, a challenge faced by parenting programme co-ordinators in the UK is to develop their core work with parents to involve young people. There are a few agencies that already integrate work with young people and other family members into their work with parents. Some examples are outlined here:

- **parallel group work** with parents' group and teenagers' group running at the same time and covering the same core elements. The Centre for Fun and Families runs a group programme for the teenagers of parents who are attending their 'Living with Teenagers' course. The six-week group programme for young people is called 'Avoiding Conflict with Adults' and includes the following core elements:

- understanding own behaviour
- anger management
- problem-solving
- avoiding offending
- managing relationships
- parallel group work.

   This cognitive behavioural programme focuses on developing young people's understanding of the factors influencing their behaviour, and initiating positive change. The course also helps young people enhance their listening and communication skills and looks at ways they can avoid conflict and feel more in control.

[Information reproduced with permission from the Centre for Fun and Families, April 2000]

- **family therapy** which involves the whole family in addressing dysfunctional processes. Solution-focused brief therapy is one approach used with the whole family. The basic principle of this model is to encourage each individual to utilise their own skills in devising strategies that will enable them to be focused on future solutions rather than on problems past. Eileen Murphy Consultants (see 'Useful Addresses') have developed a format called 'examine, repair and move on' which has been described as having a no-nonsense, empowering approach. Parents and children are encouraged to build on their strengths and set practical, realistic goals that can be achieved. Several Youth Offending Teams have been trained in this model.

- **focused family work** is a family therapy model developed by Dr Theodore Mutale to work with teenagers involved in antisocial or offending behaviour. It incorporates the solution-focused model, as well as other family therapy approaches to intervene with young people and their parents. The model focuses on the application of psychological techniques to identify and manage parental and youth risk factors (Mutale 2000).

- **parallel individual work** with teenagers could be developed to cover the core elements in tandem with their parents' programme. This would involve close liaison between parenting and youth justice workers, but we are not aware of any agencies using this model as yet.

- **video-based programmes and the CD-ROM 'Parenting Adolescents Wisely'** can be used by both parents and young people, as this can improve the way in which the skills highlighted in the programmes are implemented within families (Kumpfer and Alvarado 1998).

- **family skills training for parents and children** has been developed in the USA and involves the whole family in different group skills programmes and in family sessions to practise the skills learnt. The 'Strengthening Families' programme has been found to be effective for families with high risk factors for young people (10–14 years) in relation to substance abuse. The programme consists of fourteen consecutive, weekly sessions of two hours. Parents and children meet at the beginning of each session; they then spend time in their own groups, and a final hour in family sessions (Kumpfer and Tait 2000).

Other services for young people and their families

A range of initiatives that include early family intervention services have been developed recently, such as 'Sure Start' programmes which work with pre-school children and their families in disadvantaged areas to provide support and promote health and well-being. 'On Track'-funded projects are also being developed to promote preventative initiatives which will focus on improving opportunities for young people, their families and communities.

Next steps

As the many projects that have been set up in the last 18 months develop, it is likely that other creative ways of involving young people directly in parenting programmes will emerge. We anticipate that the support role played by TSA will include the dissemination of developments in this area of practice, as well as the other issues outlined above.

Conclusion

TSA's work as national supporters to 42 parenting projects funded by the Youth Justice Board has given us the opportunity to be part of a rapidly developing area of practice. There are as yet no evidence-based good practice standards in this field, but there is a wealth of experience and innovation being brought to bear to resolve complex issues and to provide services that are supportive and strengthening for parents and families. Some of this work is described above, but some is inevitably missing. One of our support tasks is to bring together practitioners and parenting agencies to establish a better picture of what is happening across the UK and to begin to create some practice standards. This work will link with the findings from evaluations that are taking place within projects, and with the national evaluation of the 42 projects being conducted by the Policy Research Bureau. In 2002, when these findings will be brought together, a clearer picture of effective interventions for parents should emerge.

We have outlined above the many ways in which Youth Offending Teams and their partner agencies are responding to the support needs of parents. Although the effectiveness of Parenting Orders is still open to question, there is no doubt that a more integrated approach to youth offending and antisocial behaviour is long overdue. Parents who in the past have not been able to access services can now expect some support to be available to help them and their families to deal with what, for many, can be a challenging time, and for some feels overwhelming. Some parents who have had difficult experiences but have had positive support will in turn be able to contribute their skills and experience to others. By involving young people, their parents and families in developing new models of intervention, and in assessment, planning, delivery and evaluation of services, we can help to ensure the development of more relevant and effective support into the future.

References

Brown, M. (1998) 'Recommended practices. A review of the literature on parent education and support.' Parent Education Partnership Committee of the Governor's Family Services Council, University of Delaware, June 1998. http://bluehen.ags.udel.edu/strength/best/cover.htm

Cusick, J., Lindfield, S. and Coleman, J. (2000) *Working with Parents in the Youth Justice Context.* Brighton: Trust for the Study of Adolescence.

Coleman, J., Henricson, C. and Roker, D. (1999) *Parenting in the Youth Justice Context.* Brighton: Trust for the Study of Adolescence.

Graham, J. and Bowling, B. (1995) *Young People and Crime.* London: Home Office Research Study 145.

Henggeler, S., Melton, G. and Smith, L. (1992) 'Family preservation using multisystemic therapy: An effective alternative to incarcerating serious juvenile offenders.' *Journal of Consulting and Clinical Psychology 60,* 953–961.

Henricson, C. (1998) *Support for the Parents of Adolescents.* Brighton: Trust for the Study of Adolescence.

Henricson, C., Coleman, J. and Roker, D. (2000) *Parent Assessment: A Tool for Youth Offending Teams.* Brighton: Trust for the Study of Adolescence.

Home Office (1998) *Youth Justice: The Statutory Principal Aim of Preventing Offending by Young People.* London: Home Office.

Kumpfer, K. (1993) *Strengthening America's Families: Promising Parenting and Family Strengthening Strategies for Delinquency Prevention.* Washington DC: Office of Juvenile Justice and Delinquency Prevention, US Department of Justice.

Kumpfer, K. L. and Alvarado, R. (1998) 'Effective family strengthening interventions.' *Juvenile Justice Bulletin* November 1998. Washington DC: Office of Juvenile Justice and Delinquency Prevention, US Department of Justice.

Kumpfer, K. and Tait, C. (2000) 'Family skills training for parents and children.' *Juvenile Justice Bulletin* April 2000. Washington DC: Office of Juvenile Justice and Delinquency Prevention, US Department of Justice.

Lyon, C. (2000) *Loving Smack or Lawful Assault? A Contradiction in Human Rights and Law.* London: Institute for Public Policy Research.

Mayer, G. R. (1995) 'Preventing anti-social behaviour in schools.' *Journal of Applied Behaviour Analysis 28,* 4, 467–478.

Mutale, T. (2000) *Focussed Family Work with Anti-social or Offending Youth.* Brighton: Trust for the Study of Adolescence, or from Dr Theodore Mutale, Lowther Unit, St Andrew's Hospital, Billing Road, Northampton NN1 5DG.

Smith, C. (1996) *Developing Parenting Programmes.* London: National Children's Bureau.

Utting, D., Bright, J. and Henricson, C. (1993) *Crime and the Family. Improving Child Rearing and Preventing Delinquency.* London: Family Policy Studies Centre.

Chapter 6

Providing Support Through Telephone Helplines

Dorit Braun

Introduction

Parents of teenagers are the single largest category of callers to Parentline, the freephone helpline run by Parentline Plus, comprising almost 40 per cent of callers. In many ways this is unsurprising. Parents of teenagers do not have other places where they can easily find help, information and support. Unlike parents of young children, they do not have regular contact with a health visitor, nor do they meet each other at toddler groups, nursery or at the school gates. Many parents no longer have the support of an extended family, as so many leave their home town and close relatives behind in search of work or to further their career. Moreover, the challenges facing parents of teenagers, as discussed elsewhere in this book, can make parents reluctant to seek help unless they can be sure of confidentiality. Teenagers may be engaged in behaviours that parents regard as highly problematic and/or are ashamed about, and/or are illegal, so they may well find it very difficult to discuss these behaviours openly with other parents (especially if those parents are neighbours, friends or parents of their children's friends) or with the professionals involved with their child. There is also the fear, if one seeks help from a professional, that there will be a total loss of control of the situation, and that requesting assistance is an admission of defeat.

What does Parentline offer?

Our helpline is a free service, open seven days a week. We have received significant support from the Home Office Family Policy Unit to expand the service, as part of a range of measures set out in the government's 'Supporting Families' consultation paper. Currently we can take around 100,000 calls a year, and we are expanding to be able to take 500,000 calls a year on a 24-hour service.

Callers to the helpline talk to trained and supervised volunteers, all of whom have parenting experience. Callers can offload their feelings, discuss possible strategies, receive information, and work out what, if anything, they will do next. Callers often know what they want to do next and wish to discuss it with another parent.

There are some important benefits of a helpline to parents seeking help and support. The caller is in control – they decide when to call, and can always terminate the call whenever they want to. They can call from their own home, or from another place they choose. The information they give is confidential and anonymous. They do not have to look at someone when disclosing difficult feelings, emotions and circumstances. They are not judged, but are always taken seriously and believed. They can talk things through, and obtain support that is relevant to them at that particular moment in time, rather than getting generalised information or being told what to do. They can also feel less solitary when they realise that thousands of people experience similar difficulties. And the service is free. Given the potential obstacles to seeking help facing parents of teenagers, it is clear that a telephone helpline offers an easy and accessible source of information and support.

What do parents of teenagers tell us?

In 1999 we analysed a random sample of calls from parents of teenagers, to try to gain a fuller understanding of their concerns. All calls to Parentline which involve a conversation (rather than seeking information only) generate a call return sheet that is completed by the volunteer calltaker, without reference to the name or address of the caller so as to retain confidentiality.

We studied a random sample of 43 call return sheets recording calls about teenagers received during the period July–September 1999. During this period the helpline took a total of 8028 calls, 40 per cent of which concerned teenagers. Interestingly, the numbers of boys and girls causing concern, within the total of calls concerning teenagers, are almost the same. Of the calls received during the sample period which generated call return sheets, 1092 concerned boys/young men and 1269 concerned girls/young women. During the sample period 1422 of these calls were about young people aged 13–15 (of whom 631 were male and 791 female) and 939 were about young people aged 16–18 (of whom 461 were male and 478 female). This suggests that, contrary to popular media concern about young men, parents themselves are equally concerned about their daughters.

Although a small-scale study, our analysis of 43 calls provides some valuable and interesting insights into the struggles of parents of teenagers, as well as into the particular contribution a helpline can make to supporting this group of parents.

It is important to point out that callers retain their anonymity even when cited in this sample, as many thousands of parents call us about similar issues every month. Quotes used are taken from notes made by the calltaker on the call return sheet during or straight after the call, and are thus not necessarily verbatim. Parentline is a confidential helpline and would not reveal names or addresses of callers in its research, in the rare case that these details were actually given to the calltaker.

Background information about the study

Who were the callers?

Of the 43 callers 34 were women, of whom 23 were the birth mother; additionally one caller was a birth and foster mother, four were birth and stepmothers and six callers were stepmothers.. Nine were men, of whom seven were stepfathers, one the non-resident birth father, and one the resident birth father continuing to share a house with his ex-wife. (Four were both birth and stepfather). There were 126 children in the families of these 43 callers: 73 boys/young men and 53 girls/young women.

What did they call about?

Callers raised concerns about their children, but also about their own adult relationships. They described difficult and distressing situations, and their own feelings of resentment, anger, frustration and despair.

Descriptions of teenage behaviour

The single biggest concern for callers was a range of challenging behaviour by their teenagers. The most noticeable finding from the sample was the way in which parents described their children, seeming often to have lost sight of the fact that the behaviour does not describe the person. The words most frequently used to describe teenagers include: aggressive, abusive, rebellious, spoilt, awful, out of control, violent, threatening, rude, blackmailing, provocative, controlling, resentful and antisocial. These words were used 25 times to describe the teenagers.

Other common issues and concerns were:

- school/college problems (including bullying, truancy, not working, not happy at school) – 10 calls. The high number of these calls has led us to undertake a separate study, currently underway, of all calls to the helpline concerning schooling.

- smoking – 4 calls

- drugs – 4 calls

- police involvement – 3 calls

- staying out all night – 4 calls

- sex – 3 calls

- alcohol – 2 calls

- wrong friends – 2 calls.

These numbers add up to more than 43 (including the words used in the above paragraph), because many calls concerned more than one issue or concern. In fact, this is another important aspect of the analysis, which confirms our commonsense understanding and daily experience – callers have a multiplicity of concerns, and do not divide them into neat packages which fit service delivery boundaries. (This is discussed further below.) Here, it is relevant to note that the value of a one-to-one telephone conversation with someone on our helpline is that the caller does not have to make their story fit a service, instead our service enables them to tell their story, and then to unravel the different issues and concerns, and to consider possible strategies for dealing or coping with them.

Issues mentioned once were:

- past sexual abuse
- domestic violence.

What do parents tell us about parenting issues?

Highlighted in the calls is the resentment, as well as the concern, that parents feel towards teenagers who, they feel, are making their lives difficult. Strikingly, the anger, hurt and resentment expressed by parents to volunteers on our helpline has almost no other outlets. Once parents could give vent to their feelings to an anonymous, invisible helpline volunteer, they were able to move on and start to consider what might lie behind the challenging behaviour. They were able to separate the behaviour from the child. This alone is likely to impact on the child's behaviour, as children and young people detect all too easily the feelings their parents have about them, and their behaviour can be a reflection of that.

Feedback from callers suggests that voicing difficult feelings while being supported by a trained volunteer made it possible to think about the issues from their own perspective, and from that of their teenager and others in the family. The likelihood of adults acting out their frustrations and anger on the teenagers and on other children in the family is greatly reduced when they have a safe, non-judgemental space in which to express themselves and think things through. A number of callers commented on the frustration they experienced with other services which provide only information, and said that they also needed support, and could not make use of the information unless it was applied to their own situation. They felt angry and unheard in encounters with information services.

Parents' concerns about their children's difficulties often seemed to be located in the parents' fears and concerns about their own abilities as parents to address the particular issues. It appeared from this sample that parents lacked confidence about being able to understand teenagers, lacked the skills to be able to put themselves in their teenagers' shoes, and were unable to use their own experiences of being a teenager as a way of helping themselves to understand their children.

> I feel unsure whether it is my role to discipline my stepsons when they come home later than agreed and smoke in the house, which is against the house rules. [stepfather, living with stepsons for 7 years; has 2 children of his own by the mother of his stepsons]

> My 13-year-old son is constantly threatening me but I'm afraid of arguments and crushing his confidence if I try to talk to him about it. [mother whose son has been bullied at school]

Parents need to be able to find information and understanding about the developmental processes of their children, and to have knowledge about the impact of different life stages on themselves and their children.

In this sample there were many examples of parents' lack of confidence, knowledge, understanding and skills. For example:

- 8 calls where parents found it hard to think of setting boundaries for their children

- 7 calls where parents felt that they did not know how to discipline effectively

- 6 calls where the parent had not considered the possibility of open communication and talking things through with their teenager

- 6 calls where stepparents had not recognised the need to build individual relationships with their stepchildren

- 5 calls where parents were fearful of acting on their angry feelings toward their children without the support of a helpline

- 2 calls where a parent did not make the link between their child having been bullied and the child bullying them and/or siblings

- 2 calls where what might be considered 'natural rebellion' had alarmed the parents because of their fears about where the behaviour might lead.

Most of the parents in the sample seemed to be very 'stuck' with their difficulties – with the interesting exception of lone parents, who rang before problems had escalated (see below). They described how they had 'been everywhere' and 'tried everything'. They needed time, and skilled listening and skilled questioning in order to unravel what was happening and what the real difficulties might be. They were often stuck into labelling their child, rather than their child's behaviour, and needed support to reframe the way they saw the situation and the difficulties. A major part of our work is to normalise the difficulties facing parents: often the caller feels as if they are they only person struggling, when the issue is faced by many parents. At the same time, we treat each call individually, to allow the individual to explore the particular and individual dynamics of their family and circumstances, and to consider the possible options for them. As one caller to Parentline put it when she gave us feedback about the service:

> I've been thinking over what you said to me. I realise that my son isn't behaving like this because he hates me. He's doing it because he's a teenager. And he isn't swearing deliberately to upset me. He's doing it because that's how all his friends talk – it's normal nowadays. It's really helped me to put things in perspective. [Mother of 15-year-old boy]

> I feel so much better since having that leaflet. Knowing I'm not the only one makes it more bearable. [Mother of 15-year-old boy in response to our leaflet *Parenting Teenagers*, (Parentline Plus 2000e), sent to her following a call to the helpline]

Many parents in this sample seemed resistant to the idea that they might negotiate and compromise with their teenagers, often fearing that if they 'give an inch' the teenager will 'take a mile'. Parents need opportunities to consider how they might explain their point of view and reasoning to their children, how they might be able to hear their children's point of view, and how then to work out a way through which gives everyone something of what they want, and leaves everyone feeling that the compromise is workable. To do this involves a high level of communication skills, which are, of course, a valuable asset for parents and children. However, to develop such skills requires a level of confidence and self-esteem which seemed lacking for many of the parents in this sample. Part of the difficulty is that the teenagers' behaviour in itself often has the effect of undermining parents' self-esteem, regardless of all the other life circumstances which may also rock adults' self-confidence and esteem. Many parents in this sample were living on low incomes, in low quality housing, and had previous difficulties with relationships, all of which can contribute to lowering of feelings of self-worth.

Callers to Parentline are encouraged to practise how they might approach a discussion with their teenager, and to voice their fears about what the worst outcome might be, so as to create some mental space where the idea of negotiation might be possible. However, it is clear that for many callers this will not be enough. They need more ongoing support to develop the skills needed. A call to Parentline can often leave parents willing and keen to acquire more information, understanding and skills. The experience of having been listened to and taken seriously can often open up the possibility of seeking more help and support. We do, of course, refer parents to other sources of support – but these are few and far between, as is discussed further below.

Adult concerns

For many of the parents who call us the presenting problem is about their child, but not far behind there are often concerns about adult relationships. Most calls are about several issues, and volunteers encourage callers to explore all the relevant issues by enabling them to tell their story, in their own way, before attempting to consider possible strategies for coping.

The most frequent adult concern in this study was about couple difficulties and/or parent and ex-partner disagreements and conflicts. These issues were present in 15 of the 43 calls analysed. Within this group, 7 calls were about step-couple disagreements and 6 were about disagreements with non-resident parents/ex-partners. We are planning a separate study of calls about couple difficulties, in order to understand better what callers are telling us about their adult relationships.

Other adult concerns frequently mentioned were:

- ill health, disability, mental health problems, alcohol use problems – 12 calls
- domestic violence, fear of hurting children – 6 calls
- loneliness – 5 calls
- dislike of children – 6 calls
- low income/threat to benefits – 4 calls
- lack of control – 3 calls
- difficulties caused by summer holiday period – 3 calls.

Other issues less frequently mentioned were:

- legal position of stepparent in sole charge of children
- non-resident father cut off from children
- previous abuse of caller
- stepfather unsure of his role
- stepfather finding stepdaughter sexually provocative.

What do callers tell us about their lives?

An interesting aspect of this study is how it reveals the complexities and intricacies of family life. In the real world, rather than a world designed by service providers, people do not separate their concerns about their adult lives and relationships from their concerns about their children. These concerns are intertwined. And of course, a parent who is struggling in a relationship where he or she feels unsupported, or is struggling with financial or health problems, is much more likely to find any challenge from their child harder to cope with. Moreover, the child may well be behaving in challenging ways because she or he has picked up on other concerns and difficulties in the family, and may be 'acting out' his or her anxieties about these difficulties. It also seems that for callers to Parentline, it is more acceptable to seek help for a parenting difficulty than for a couple or relationship difficulty. Many of the callers in this sample had tried other sources of help before ringing us (see below), but had always focused their search for help on managing their child's behaviour.

Men and women as callers

Overall, around 80 per cent of callers to Parentline are women, and the majority of them are in intact relationships. However, it was noticeable in this sample that all the male callers were separated or in a second (step) family. There are possible reasons for this. Men in contact with us seem to need a 'good reason' to seek help. It could be that their experience of previous relationship breakdown makes them more anxious about this happening again and therefore willing to seek support. For men in a stepfamily, it could also be that they are taking a more active role in helping to manage the life of the family because it is possible for them to negotiate a 'nontraditional' role when setting up a new family. Other research suggests that men in stepfamilies are more actively involved in family life than men in intact families (Ferri and Smith 1998; Wilson 1996). Of course, it is also very important that the service is promoted in such a way as to make it clear that it is for fathers as well as mothers.

Stepfamily issues

From the evidence of this sample, many of the issues encountered by birth families and stepfamilies are similar. However, the difficulties can often feel greater to adults and children in stepfamilies, because of the complexity of the numbers of people in a stepfamily, the divided and conflicting loyalties, and the different histories and values owned by members of a stepfamily.

> I feel as if I'm a lodger in my own house; the way my husband's sons manipulate him is threatening our relationship. [stepmother, fearing that if the difficulties are addressed her husband will support his sons, not her]

Work with young people undertaken by Parentline Plus (Smith 2000), as well as other research, suggests that children and young people can feel rushed into accepting a parent's new partner without being given time to adjust to the changes, and time to get to know the adult who is coming into their lives. Parents and stepparents caught up in their new relationship can overlook the unsettling impact it may be having on their children, and on their children's behaviour (Neale and Smart 1998; Parentline Plus 2000d).

Lone parent issues

> How do other people cope in my situation? I feel so alone.

In this sample, it seems that the issues facing lone parents are similar to those facing all parents. However, the most noticeable difference in this sample was that lone parents called earlier, before problems and difficulties had escalated. The involvement of external family members and friends did not feature for most callers in this sample, so in a household with only one adult it seems that lone parents use Parentline as a sounding board in helping to think through issues and strategies.

Using other services

Many of the callers in this sample had tried other agencies for help and support; schools and GPs were most frequently mentioned, but did not appear to have helped callers. For example, one caller was told that the health service could not help her as hers was not a medical problem. Other services, including Court Welfare and other information helplines, had not been perceived as helpful by callers in this sample, because they did not offer emotional support as part of the service. In two cases parents had sought referrals for their child and had been signposted to a number of agencies, including the police, solicitors and social services, before finding an appropriate referral, which their children then refused to use. In other calls parents were afraid to seek help from statutory agencies, specifically because they feared being fined as a result of their child's refusal to attend school.

Worryingly, some parents in the sample said that they had sought help so as not to act out their anger and frustration on their children. This has serious implications for the way support is provided if children are to be properly protected. Agencies who offer only information need a strong awareness that this may not be enough for a parent under stress, who needs support as well as information. And agencies who try not to take on new clients need a good enough assessment process to ensure that they enable parents really to express and articulate their concerns before they decide whether or not they can offer them a service.

It seems that for parents there are a number of difficulties with local services. Part of the problem is that parents do not know about most services, even when these exist, and so turn to schools and GPs, who at least appear to provide a universal service. But teachers and GPs do not have time to provide meaningful emotional support to parents – although it would help parents greatly if they were not pushed aside or brushed off, but instead told where else they could go. Parentline Plus is attempting to ensure that schools and GP surgeries hold details of our helpline to give to parents.

A related problem is that parents need time and support to tell their story and get to the bottom of the real difficulties. The presenting issue or problem may not turn out to be the most pressing concern – it may simply be the concern that the parents find easiest to talk about, or acceptable to ring a helpline about, or the concern that seems at the time to be most pressing. Only with the help of skilled questioning and listening can parents work out what is really bothering them and what, if anything, they want to do about it. This is a central part of helpline work, and involves skilled listening and communications work. Many professionals do not have either the time or the skills needed for this. Related to this is the tendency of services to provide help around boundaries that they define, which may be too narrow or too simplistic for many parents experiencing interconnected difficulties. So teachers work on schooling and related issues – but not on general support – but, ironically, it may not be possible for parents and children to give any real attention to the schooling issues until they get emotional support for the issues as they see them. To make matters worse, many services are desperately stretched, unable to meet all the local demand, and so have a tendency to look for reasons why parents do not qualify for their service, rather than looking to ways in which they could help them.

Involvement of other family members and friends

For most of the calls in this sample, a support network of family members and friends did not feature; perhaps this is why people rang us, or perhaps it is related to the scale of couple disagreements in these calls, where couples in conflict are loath to involve other people for fear of further problems with conflicting loyalties. Callers also contact us because they don't want to talk to, or upset, family members and friends; they may also be ashamed of what is happening and fear a judgmental response from people they know. Occasionally callers were disappointed at the lack of support from relatives who lived close by. In some cases our volunteer was able to help the caller identify a friend or family member from whom they could get some social support – e.g. go away with, or have a night out with. The absence of social networks, which is likely to have contributed to people's loneliness and sense of isolation, is a feature of these calls, and when people feel isolated it is especially hard to have a sense of balance or proportion about perceived parenting difficulties. For this reason, we believe it is of critical importance to make information about parenting widely available, through the mass media, so that anyone parenting a child comes across information that helps them recognise that they are not alone, and is enabled to access relevant information. We used the analysis of these 43 calls to launch a media campaign in partnership with BT on the importance of communication in families, and will continue to give considerable time, resource and energy to ensuring that information about parenting features is disseminated in the mass media.

What further help do parents need?

The analysis of these 43 calls highlights the importance of the support parents need so that they can continue to 'be there' for their teenage children. Some parents may have a network of family and friends who can help them with that, but for parents in this sample such a network did not appear to be a significant feature of their lives. Other research, commissioned by Parentline Plus from Anglia Polytechnic University to examine what parents need from a helpline, found that around 10 per cent of parents described themselves as having no-one to turn to for help and support. And this figure was noticeably higher in an area of social and economic disadvantage, where 19 per cent of parents said they had no-one to turn to (Akister and Johnson 2000). There are very few local free services offering parents a confidential space in which to offload their feelings, get support and increase their skills and confidence. Work is starting on a number of innovative projects to support parents of teenagers, as a result of a number of government initiatives, including the introduction of parenting orders as part of the reform of the youth justice system, and the funding of innovative projects and services by the Home Office Family Support Unit grants programme in 2000–2001.

It was clear from this analysis that calling Parentline is an important and accessible starting point to seeking assistance or support for parents of teenagers, but that for many parents more help is needed. Callers in this sample needed help with a number of key communications issues and skills, including:

- identifying life cycle changes and their impact for themselves and for their children
- setting up and renegotiating age-appropriate and achievable boundaries
- managing change, including divorce, separation, setting up a new (step-)family, moving schools
- identifying other useful adults and asking for appropriate help and support
- listening to young people
- keeping in touch with young people's situations and concerns
- negotiating and resolving conflicts.

Parentline Plus runs a network of parenting courses which help to develop the communications skills needed by parents of teenagers, and we are working to expand the availability of these courses. We are also developing new materials for running courses for parents of teenagers, as well as working to identify good practice and produce good practice guidance. We are working with Youth Offending Teams to develop courses specific to parents in the youth justice context, and have developed information leaflets for parents whose teenagers are 'in trouble' (Parentline Plus 2000a–c).

In response to the lack of confidential and anonymous services available to parents, and the obvious benefits of providing support on the telephone, we are currently piloting a new telephone support service, which will offer parents more than a one-off call. This new service offers parents a weekly call from the same telephone supporter over an eight-week period, thus offering ongoing support. The aim is to support the parent to work on agreed goals and targets during that period. It seems clear that many parents need more than one phone call, but that local services are very hard to access, and/or that parents prefer to have the control as well as the anonymity offered by a telephone service. Interestingly, as part of the feasibility study to develop this new service, we consulted with potential service users, all of whom were either now subject to Parenting Orders or were clients of a social services department. Without exception, all the parents we consulted had sought help many years earlier, before their children were teenagers, but had been told that their situation was not serious enough to provide social services input. It is clear that parents themselves do want help early on – the challenge is to make it available in accessible and acceptable ways. This is a challenge for all of us in the family and parenting support field.

Comments and conclusions

A telephone helpline alone cannot provide all the support needed by parents of teenagers. Much more is needed, and many agencies, statutory and voluntary, have an important contribution to make to provide accessible and appropriate support. The lessons from this research suggest that agencies need to devote attention to really listening to parents and exploring with them the nature of their concerns, before jumping in to offer information, solutions or advice, or saying that they cannot provide a service. This requires skills and time, which many agencies do not have. In the absence of these, at a minimum, services for children and families should at least know about other support services – local and national – so that they can refer parents to these.

However, callers to Parentline confirm the value of a confidential telephone service. The service can allow people time, and can provide a starting point for them to resolve their difficulties themselves, which includes providing them with information about how to use other services, and how to find them. When parents ring Parentline they feel able to say what in any other part of their lives would be 'unsayable'. Being allowed to say the 'unsayable' allows parents to explore their feelings. It also opens up their options and potential courses of action. These may include confronting and dealing with their difficulties, taking more time for themselves, taking some time to consider different options and strategies and which feels best for them, contacting another agency, holding a family meeting, attending a parenting course, etc. Callers said that voicing difficult feelings while being supported made it easier to think about the issues from different perspectives. Some callers talked about how, by describing their fears and feelings, the heat was taken out of a situation. The likelihood of them taking out their frustrations on their children was greatly reduced because they had a safe, non-judgemental space in which to think things through.

It is clear from our work that the essence of many parents' anxieties has often been missed in past face-to-face experiences with professionals. The problem gets looked at, but they, as human beings, seem to feel invisible. In contrast, when they are invisible, on the other end of a telephone, they finally feel heard. We know that children need to be listened to and heard, and given opportunities to participate actively in decisions about their lives. The same is true for their parents. Parents need to feel heard, understood and supported in order to offer the same to their children.

Note

This chapter draws from research undertaken by Cheryl Walters, Head of Policy and Research at Parentline Plus, and published as a briefing paper 'Saying the Unsayable', Summer 1999.

References

Akister, J. and Johnson, K. (April 2000) 'What do parents want from a confidential helpline?' (Commissioned by Parentline Plus.) Anglia Polytechnic University.

Ferri, E. and Smith, K. (1998) *Step-parenting in the 90s*. London: Family Policy Studies Centre.

Neale, B. and Smart, C. (1998) *Family Fragments*. Cambridge: Polity Press.

Resources available from Parentline Plus

Parentline Plus (supported by the Youth Justice Board) (2000a) *A parent's easy guide to going to court with your child.* Leaflet available through Parentline Plus.

Parentline Plus (supported by the Youth Justice Board) (2000b) *A parent's easy guide to acting as an appropriate adult.* Leaflet available through Parentline Plus.

Parentline Plus (supported by the Youth Justice Board) (2000c) *A parent's easy guide to Parenting Orders.* Leaflet available through Parentline Plus.

Parentline Plus (2000d) *Stepfamilies – challenges, myths and rewards.* Leaflet available through Parentline Plus.

Parentline Plus (2000e) *Parenting teenagers. A survival guide for mums and dads.* Leaflet available through Parentline Plus.

Smith, C. (2000) *Children, Young People and Family Change – Their Shout.* Parentline Plus. Available through Parentline Plus.

Wilson, L. (1996) *Diary of a Stepfather.* Parentline Plus. Available through Parentline Plus.

Chapter 7

Using the Parent Adviser Model to Support Parents of Teenagers

Hilton Davis and Crispin Day

Introduction

> *Your children are not your children.*
> *They are the sons and daughters of Life's longing for itself.*
> *They come through you but not from you.*
> *And though they are with you yet they belong not to you.*
>
> *You may give them your love but not your thoughts,*
> *For they have their own thoughts...*
> *You may strive to be like them, but seek not to make them like you.*

Khalil Gibran (1992)

Children are separate individuals from birth, and the role for parents is to adapt to and nurture this uniqueness – usually without explicit preparation. This demanding task is essentially a continual attempt to understand what the child is doing, thinking and feeling, so as to respond appropriately. It is complicated, however, by the fact that children and young people are involved in a process of change, which accelerates in the teenage years, where one's understanding as a parent may often lag behind their developmental progress.

Given the complexity of the task and the demands upon parents to change and adapt, the role can be stressful, particularly in contexts where other stresses impinge. In deprived inner-city areas, for example, where high numbers of parents face poverty, social isolation, family breakdown, poor housing, environmental threats and personal mental health difficulties (Davis, Day, Cox and Cutler 2000; Attride-Stirling et al. 2000), the need for help is evident. A random community survey (Davis et al. 2000), for example, found that the number of psychosocial problems parents described in their children increased with age. Fifty-two per cent of parents of 11– 13-year-olds described their children as having three or more problems, compared to 20.9 per cent for 0–4-year-olds and 35.2 per cent for 5–10s. Whatever the level of problems, 25 per cent of the parents felt that they needed help, as did 19 per cent of the teenagers in the study by Attride-Stirling et al. (2000).

Such evidence indicates very high levels of need for support in families. But where do they go for help? One obstacle is a general reluctance to seek help, because such problems can be perceived as a reflection of one's own inadequacy. Parenting tends to be construed as natural, and any difficulties are frequently attributed to or blamed on the parents, without taking into account the individuality of the child, the uniqueness of the interaction between the parent and child, and the whole context of their relationship.

To seek help requires a measure of trust in the person from whom help is requested, and friends and relatives are, therefore, likely to be the first port of call, if available. However, they may be no more knowledgeable than the parents, and may jump to solutions without appropriate exploration of all the issues. They may also be involved in the problem by way of their relationship with the parent and may not be able to think clearly about it.

An alternative is to approach local professionals, such as GPs, health visitors or teachers. However, they may not have been trained to deal with child and family problems and may feel pressured to give solutions quickly without listening to the parents fully and engaging the knowledge, skills, experience and qualities of the parents themselves (Davis and Fallowfield 1991). In some areas parenting courses are becoming available, but they are rarely specific to the parents of teenagers and are not systematically available to the whole population.

A further option for help is the more specialist child and adolescent mental health services, although resources are limited and not easily accessible. Families usually have to be referred, often to centres some way from home, with long waiting times (Audit Commission 1999). In practice, few parents manage to see mental health specialists, and those that do have generally had the problem for more than a year before being seen; 69.4 per cent, according to unpublished data by Davis et al. (1998). The absence of resources makes the likelihood of promotional, preventive or early intervention work remote (Mental Health Foundation 1999).

To make help more accessible, the NHS Health Advisory Service (1995) has suggested services be organised on a tiered basis of increasing specialisation. Putting this into practice, Day, Davis and Hind (1998) have been attempting to train all staff (e.g. health visitors, teachers, school nurses, community paediatricians) working routinely with families to be able to provide more effective psychological and social support. This is Tier 1 of an integrated service and it requires that community personnel be selected, trained and supported appropriately to carry out this psychosocial role. Such training and subsequent supervision is provided by solo child mental health specialists (Tier 2) based in community localities and working closely with all other disciplines. These specialists may also see families themselves in GP surgeries or schools, when the families' needs are higher than can be managed by Tier 1. Families with even higher levels of need, requiring specific expertise, for example, or that of several specialists simultaneously (e.g. child psychotherapy, psychiatry, psychology), may be referred to Tier 3 (i.e. generic multidisciplinary child and adolescent mental health teams), or to Tier 4, which consists of highly specialist teams (e.g. inpatient units) dealing with the most severe and least common disorders.

The development of Tier 1 requires considerable change in policy (e.g. to include psychosocial problems as significant), in management (e.g. selecting and supporting staff for a more general helping role) and in resources, because time is needed to enable such help to occur. Most important, however, is the need for accessible models or guidance on how to provide such help, the training to deliver it, and subsequent supervision, because of the complexities inherent in dealing with psychosocial issues.

It is this role that the parent adviser model is intended to fulfil. It is not a denial of the knowledge and expertise of health, education, social service or voluntary agency staff, but rather a statement of the psychological or human nature of the helping process. All helping is founded on psychological and social processes that are rarely given the importance they require; giving advice or prescribing drugs are always based upon communication and interpersonal relationships. Although these are important in determining outcome, they are often poorly understood by professionals, not applied skilfully in practice, and the source of considerable dissatisfaction for parents (Davis and Fallowfield 1991).

In this chapter we will begin with a general outline of the parent adviser model by describing and illustrating its theoretical underpinnings. We will then discuss the training, service implications (especially in relation to the teenage years) and the evidence for the effectiveness of the approach. The ideas are presented to stimulate careful consideration of the core processes of helping with the intention of enabling partnerships between professions, between helpers and parents, between parents, and between parents and their children/teenagers.

Parent adviser model: basic theory

The parent adviser model derives originally from work with parents of children with disabilities (e.g. Buchan, Clemerson and Davis 1988; Cunningham and Davis 1985). Services in the early 1980s tended to focus almost exclusively on children's health and development, paying little attention to the child's emotional wellbeing and quality of life. The problems of the parents in adapting to the child's difficulties were usually of incidental importance to those of the children, if not ignored entirely. In reality, however, parents are the most important element in the helping process. If they do not turn up at the clinic or are not at home for a visit, professionals can do nothing for the child. If the parents disagree with professionals, do not understand instructions, do not have the practical resources required (time, money and space) or the psychological resources, they are unlikely to comply, and the potential of professional help for their child will be reduced. For these reasons, the importance of parents' needs must be acknowledged. This is true for all problems, including those concerning the behaviour of their teenagers. They control all help for their children, and their emotional adaptation should be of primary concern to all potential helpers. Their involvement or partnership in the process is crucial, not only because of the significant distress caused by their teenagers' problems, but also because the parents' own behaviour may be causing, increasing or maintaining problems in their children.

Helping is not, therefore, just about knowing the skills of parenting and imparting this to parents; it includes a much more complex process of communication. To be effective, helpers must get to know and be trusted by parents in a way that enables the helper's ideas to be tailored to the existing expertise and resources of the parents, the specific characteristics of their teenagers, and their general situation. Since few helpers have ever covered the theory and skills involved in these communication processes in their basic or even advanced training, the parent adviser model was developed and elaborated to compensate for the omission. It involved: (1) the derivation of relatively simple theoretical frameworks to enable helpers to understand and to guide their interaction with parents; and (2) the development of a training course to explore the frameworks and to practise the associated skills. The theoretical ideas are briefly described below.

Adaptation

The basis of the theoretical framework is a general model of how parents function and adapt, and was alluded to in the introduction to this chapter. It derives from personal construct theory (Kelly 1955), the underlying theme of which is that all people are like scientists, devising, testing and developing theories to enable them to understand, anticipate and hence adapt to the events of their world. The basic assumption is that what we do is determined by the ways in which we make sense of our world and what happens to us, although unlike scientists' theories, our theories (or construct systems) are neither explicitly stated nor, necessarily, conscious. The model assumes that parents are constantly involved in an active process of constructing a unique model of their world on the basis of their own individual experience. One might think of it as painting in the mind a complex picture of the world as it impinges on us as individuals. The picture includes the physical objects and events we encounter, as well as ourselves and our experiences with all the people with whom we have contact.

Teenagers, just like parents, are also involved in the same processes, and growing up can be seen as the rapid development of an individual's unique set of constructs about the world, which evolves as the child gets older. The interaction between parents and teenagers can, therefore, be seen as an ongoing, moment-to-moment attempt by two people to make sense of the construct of the other. The parent of a moody teenager is engaged in: (1) monitoring what the teenager says and does; (2) interpreting (i.e. construing) what the child is intending, meaning or feeling; and (3) using this to anticipate how to respond. The parent's response is in turn: (1) monitored by the teenager, who (2) attempts to interpret or make sense of the parent's response, and (3) uses this as the basis for how to respond (or not).

Interaction will be unproblematic, as long as the parent and child construe the world similarly. However, there will be problems related to the extent to which their constructions differ, and this might be more frequent in adolescence. A mother's concern for her son, expressed as, 'You're looking tired', may be construed otherwise by the teenager and elicit a response of, 'Leave me alone; you're always getting at me'. Their interactions will be more difficult when the parents or teenagers are, for example, preoccupied by other problems or issues and are not listening to each other. Seeing one's role as a parent as having to control the child in relation to all aspects of his/her development and learning may also prevent effective interaction. It prohibits construing the teenager as the separate, self-determining individual described in Gibran's lines at the beginning of this chapter. This may lead parents into an inconsiderate, conflictual or coercive style of interaction, as opposed to a relationship based upon respect and negotiation.

The model of parenting implied here is one of providing the conditions (time, circumstance and relationship) in which one can listen to the young person, negotiate a reasonable understanding and develop a way of being together that meets the needs of both. It implies a process that is not unlike the model of the general helping process, which is described next.

The helping process

Given that problems in parenting can be seen as related to how we construe the world, it follows that a major aim of helping is to understand how parents currently construe their situation, and to enable them to make appropriate or useful changes. This process can be seen as a series of stages or tasks, described below.

ESTABLISHING A RELATIONSHIP

The process begins with the development of a relationship between helper and parent. This is a vital task, helpful in itself, and a prerequisite of all the other stages. If parents do not like, trust or respect the helper, the process will founder. Parents may benefit from the helper's knowledge and expertise, but not if it is provided in ways that disempower them and take away their self-esteem and efficacy.

The aim of the helper is, therefore, to develop a partnership in which there is equality and mutual respect, where helper and parent work closely together, pooling their expertise, agreeing aims and strategies, and negotiating flexibly wherever there is potential conflict. Such a relationship is of benefit in itself, since by being respected by someone they value and with whom they genuinely share the power in the relationship, parents will be empowered and hence better equipped to meet the inevitable challenges of parenting. However, being in such a partnership facilitates the helping process generally, because it initiates a creative situation in which ideas, strategies and solutions can be shared in mutual trust, honesty and openness. The more parents feel understood, the more the relationship can develop, the better they are likely to feel, and the more the process will be facilitated.

EXPLORATION

The next task, which inevitably overlaps with developing a relationship, involves a careful exploration of the problems presented by the parent. Jumping to solutions is unlikely to be successful, unless there is a clear picture of the problem and the issues involved. This can be relatively simple and quick, or may take a considerable time if the number and severity of the problems require a detailed exploration of the parents' construction system, including their general philosophy and values, their relationships and their own characteristics, as well as the specific problems.

The process involves the helper in trying to see the parents' world, eliciting their constructions, and not imposing his/her own. This requires careful listening, questioning and discussion, leading to a clear view of the parent's picture or constructions, which, like hypotheses, can then be tested. This requires the helper to build up a picture of the world as expressed by the parent, but at the same time to compare it with the helper's own picture. For example, in exploring her concerns, a mother explained her daughter's constant defiance in terms of her (the mother's) own inadequacies as a parent. In listening to what she was saying and having met the daughter, the helper accepted the mother's view as a hypothesis, but also developed an alternative hypothesis, that the defiance resulted from the daughter's own dissatisfaction with herself. Armed with both pictures, the helper's task was to challenge the mother's view carefully and tentatively, so that a more accurate picture might result. She did this without implying the superiority of her own view over the mother's, but by suggesting that there might be alternative explanations that should be compared and tested. In this case, it led to the mother engaging her daughter in a calm conversation in which both possibilities were compared and explored, leading to a much more complicated explanation that centred on the daughter's own self-esteem and her estranged father's criticism.

CLARIFICATION

Such exploration is not a diagnostic process in which an attempt is simply made to discover what is wrong from the expert helper's point of view. It is a social activity in which two people work together to reach a shared understanding of what has happened, with as much concern for what is right in the situation (including a discovery of the parents' and teenager's strengths) as for what is wrong. The intention is to produce greater clarity in the parents' understanding. We see this as a specific stage or task, because it is not only the basis for further stages, it can be extremely helpful in itself.

Understanding, for example, reduces anxiety, and can be a relief, even when there is little one can do to change a situation. It might eliminate unnecessary and inappropriate shame or guilt, by, for example, realising that one is not necessarily to blame for what has happened. For these and other reasons, the helping process could stop here and still have been useful to the parents in reaching acceptance (e.g. in a bereavement situation) or feeling able to go on to find solutions for themselves. Through discussion, a father who was concerned about his relationship with his daughter changed from a construction of her as deliberately excluding him, to understanding that this was about her awakening sexuality. This insight was sufficient for him no longer to require help.

SETTING GOALS

A clear model provides the basis from which to approach the next stage, which is the formulation of aims and goals. This is such an important stage, since helpers and parents may differ considerably in their aims, and it is the aims that determine possible solutions. It is, therefore, important for the helper to address the issue of aims explicitly and to elicit clearly what the parents would like to achieve.

This involves further exploration, and even negotiation, if the two disagree, but it also requires consideration of multiple goals, priorities, and subgoals. For example, in discussing what a mother should do to help her teenage son, who was constantly complaining of ill health and not going to school, it was decided that the first aims were to involve him in the decision-making process, in order that he might take at least partial responsibility for attending school. Further exploration, however, made it clear that a first step would have to be to obtain the agreement of her husband, who, she predicted, would not agree to the son taking any responsibility, because of strong authoritarian views about parents being the decision-makers.

PLANNING STRATEGIES

Once clear goals are agreed, then it is possible to move to the next step of devising strategies or solutions. The creation of strategies is easier if the goals are well formulated (e.g. clear, specific and concrete). The process of finding solutions should continue to be a partnership, with the helper and parents combining their ideas. This does not prohibit experienced helpers from making suggestions about what parents might do, but parents should still be involved in the process, ideally producing ideas themselves. The helper's solutions may impress the parents, who might be relieved and grateful, but if the ideas are generated by the parents, then: 1) their confidence will also be increased; 2) their understanding and acceptance of the ideas are more likely; 3) they are more likely to do what they think is right, and 4) to have a greater sense of achievement.

The role for the parent adviser is to try to elicit suggestions from parents, and to explore and develop these together. Whoever makes the initial suggestion, careful planning is crucial, and all potential strategies need to be considered in detail for their feasibility. One option is to brainstorm as many different strategies as possible together, and to then compare them and decide the most effective, even combining them if appropriate. If possible this should involve a very detailed consideration of exactly what should be done, when, where, by whom and how, trying to predict likely obstacles and difficulties, even practising skills that parents might require. This is illustrated by the case of a distraught mother who could not bring herself to tell her 14 year old son that his estranged father had been murdered. Discussion with the school nurse led to a decision that he should be told and that the mother should do it herself. Detailed preparation included role-playing specific sentences that she might use, with help from a book on breaking bad news, discovered by the mother.

IMPLEMENTATION

Once plans have been made as carefully as possible, the next step is, of course, to carry them out. However, even if this is the parent's responsibility, the helper should be accessible for support. This might vary from simple encouragement and praise, to monitoring the situation generally, and discussing unforeseen difficulties and adjusting the strategy to compensate. The value for parents of someone they trust and with whom they can share the situation cannot be overestimated.

EVALUATION

The final stage is that of evaluating the outcomes of the implemented strategies, with the helper and parents exploring the degree of success. If successful, the role of the helper is to praise and congratulate the parent, ensuring that responsibility for success is taken as much as possible by the parents. It might also be important to consider the reasons for success and the light these might shed on why the difficulties arose in the first place, and how they might be avoided in future.

Very much the same process should occur even if the strategies were not entirely successful. Encouragement for the parents is essential within a careful analysis of why the strategy did not work. This might have been, for example, because there were unforeseen problems in implementation, the goals were unrealistic, or the reasons for the problems had not, in retrospect, been totally understood. Whatever the reasons, the evaluation should involve backtracking on the process we have described, exploring the situation further, being clearer in understanding it, resetting goals and rethinking the strategy. In essence the process is one in which hypotheses are being set up and tested by means of strategies that can be construed as mini-experiments.

Helper qualities and skills

If such a process is to be successful, it requires certain skills and qualities in both the parents and helpers. Focusing here only on the skills of the helper, the parent adviser model has been heavily influenced by Rogers (e.g. 1959), who assumes that if the helper is able to demonstrate certain general qualities, parents are more likely to be engaged in an effective relationship, to work through the helping processes, to change and to be effective. We will illustrate the most important qualities, which can be understood variously as a set of attitudes, a general stance towards people seeking help, or superordinate constructions that are likely to have large effects upon the ways in which we interact and communicate with parents.

RESPECT

This is an overriding view of other people as significant and of value. It means being positive and non-judgemental, assuming competence and strength in parents, assuming that they can take responsibility, can help themselves and make significant changes to their lives. It also involves making them the absolute focus of your attention while with them.

Without this the helping process will fail. A police officer treating a young offender and his family with complete disdain achieves nothing, except to communicate what they might already be thinking of themselves. It does nothing to engage them, to initiate a relationship, or to facilitate the process of change.

Respect does not require you necessarily to like someone, but parents have to be persuaded that you are at least listening to them, and that you are worthy of their interest and have something to offer. You cannot force parents to relate to you, or to change. Dominating them simply reinforces their own inadequacies. Serving them, however, with humility, and assuming their importance, may eventually persuade most parents to engage with you.

GENUINENESS

This is, again, a complex characteristic. It denotes honesty, sincerity and absence of deception, and it implies that the person is to be trusted. Without trust, communication will founder and the helping process cannot occur. This is why confidentiality is such an important aspect of helping.

Respect, or any of the other qualities, cannot be perceived as such, unless they are genuine. Any hint of pretence will be picked up quickly and will undermine the helping process. However, it is impossible to be genuine towards others if one is deceiving oneself or otherwise distorting one's constructions of the world. Genuineness, therefore, involves an absence of self-deception, an openness to the world with as little distortion as possible. Without this the next characteristic would be impossible.

EMPATHY

This can be defined as an attempt to see the world from another's viewpoint. The helping process must begin from the viewpoint of the person with the problem. Unless their constructions are clear, little can be done to change the situation. Their views need not accord with your own or be accurate. What matters is that you attempt to understand the person's viewpoint fully, so that you can then work on it together and, if necessary, produce change. It is particularly important for the helping relationship that the helper be seen as interested and attempting to understand, which in turn indicates respect.

HUMILITY

Humility is a strength, not a weakness. It is a general stance that indicates that one is realistic and open about one's expertise and limitations. It allows the helper to feel uncertainty and tentativeness. This counters self-importance in the role of helper and prevents defensiveness. A genuine attitude of humility allows for the contribution of the parent, countering the illusion that the professional is all-knowing and all-powerful. It makes the helper approachable and reduces potential power barriers, thus facilitating equality and partnership.

QUIET ENTHUSIASM/WARMTH

Helpers should be warm, constructive and positive in general. The most effective helpers look for and comment upon the positive. In a ten-minute period, a project worker genuinely praised or thanked a mother and father for the care bestowed on their house; the father's handling of a problem with their son's teacher (he did not get angry); their attempt to understand their son; and their positiveness towards each other. This counteracts the vulnerability that goes with problems; it increases self-esteem; and it enhances the helping relationship by, for example, allowing the negative to be confronted more easily if necessary.

INTEGRITY

This is the final helper quality, and refers to the capacity to be strong enough to support those who are vulnerable, to tolerate the anxieties of the helping situation, and to take a reasonable, independent viewpoint. It also enables helpers to challenge parents and not just provide passive support. Although it is important to elicit and respect the constructions of the parent, helpers should try to formulate their own picture, so that comparisons may be made and change facilitated by appropriate challenges when necessary.

COMMUNICATION SKILLS

Demonstrating these qualities is likely to facilitate effective communication between the helper and parents. However, specific skills are needed to communicate with parents and to facilitate the process. The most important is the ability to listen effectively and actively. This is a complex activity, which can be improved by training.

Other skills involve the ability to prompt people to explore their worries (e.g. by appropriate questioning), to indicate understanding and to clarify (e.g. by empathic statements and summarising), to challenge people to change (e.g. by invitation and hypothesis), to resolve conflict (e.g. by negotiation) and to be creative (e.g. brainstorming and evaluating). These are described in a variety of sources (Burnard 1989; Davis 1993; Dickson, Hargie and Morrow 1989; Egan 1990) and will not be described further here.

COMPETENCE/KNOWLEDGE

The qualities discussed above complement the knowledge and expertise of the helper, and do not replace it. One should have an understanding of child development, families, helpful techniques and available services before one can be effective, and such knowledge should grow with experience, service developments and research findings.

Particularly important are theories and skills of parenting that are made explicit via the different parenting approaches that are developing rapidly in the UK and elsewhere. These are covered elsewhere in the present book and will not be discussed further here.

The parent adviser model (of adaptation, the process of helping and the qualities and skills) has been presented as a guide for helpers in working with parents. It is, however, also applicable to effective, direct communication with teenagers by independent helpers or parents. It relates directly to parenting in suggesting, for example, that the parent–teenager relationship might be somewhat more effective if seen as a partnership and not as an expert imparting wisdom to the ignorant. Listening to one's teenage children, showing respect, empathy, genuineness, warmth and humility, is likely to enhance the relationship, to indicate value and understanding, and to allow effective communication. Having trained as a parent adviser, a health visitor described how she had used exactly the same skills when her own daughter became angry and upset with her one evening. She was able to listen carefully to her without feeling too threatened by her angry criticisms, eventually discovering that her real concerns were to do with problems in her relationship with her boyfriend.

Training

On the basis of these ideas we have developed courses that allow people to explore the models and to experiment with the implications. They provide the opportunity to practise the qualities and skills in a safe environment (Davis, Cox, Day *et al.* 2000).

The basic course consists of 12 half-day sessions, held at weekly intervals because of the intellectual and emotional demands of the course and the need for reflection and assimilation throughout. It is usually run by 2 facilitators with 12 participants. In addition, there are a number of modules, each amounting to between 4 and 6 sessions. One or more of these can be integrated into the basic course to enable participants to explore specific areas and techniques. Modules have been, or are being, developed for: identification of family need and prevention in the perinatal period; post-natal depression; and parenting in infancy, middle childhood or adolescence.

An important characteristic of the course is that it attempts to demonstrate what is being trained. For example, the facilitators demonstrate the helping qualities throughout and attempt to engage in a partnership with the participants by following a process of mutual exploration, clarification and development of the participants' constructions, qualities and skills. The process begins with ideas, qualities and skills that participants bring to the course, which proceeds at their pace. Constant participation is required of the whole group, and is achieved via Socratic dialogue and not lecturing. Each session begins with a group discussion in which a question is presented (e.g. What characterises an effective helper–parent relationship?) and explored in an attempt to develop a comprehensive and detailed answer from the participants. The role of the facilitator is to engage them in an interesting conversation, to solicit, respect and organise their answers, to challenge their ideas, and to formulate an agreed model. This is followed by small-group skills practices in which participants put into practice and experiment with the ideas discussed. There are reading and practical exercises between sessions to ensure further exploration and assimilation.

Service implications

Many people from all the major professional and voluntary groups have now successfully completed the course and are likely to be more effective, whatever their role (e.g. health visitor, teacher, doctor). It is predicted that they will apply their pre-existing knowledge and expertise more effectively, without undermining parents' own strengths, yet enhancing their self-esteem and empowering them to deal with their children more ably. We also assume that they will be able to offer a broader service, relating not only to health or education, for example, but to psychosocial issues generally and parenting.

However, new skills have to be nurtured and supported once learnt, or they may be lost. For example, there may be insufficient time allocated for practising the new skills, antagonism from colleagues to new methods, or no one with whom to consider implementation difficulties and worries, or from whom to obtain encouragement and evaluative feedback. Communication and human relationships are complex and it is very easy for helpers not to know the best course of action, to feel they are failing, or to lose perspective on their effectiveness. Consequently, there is a need for regular supervision and support for anyone who is working with other people in the helping professions, and the parent adviser model includes at least one hour for this on an individual basis, at least once a fortnight.

A number of services have now been set up using professionals and volunteers as dedicated parent advisers, and including regular supervision. The first was established in London in Tower Hamlets, where a range of people (mainly health visitors and physiotherapists) were trained to provide regular support for families with children with severe disabilities (Buchan, Clemerson and Davis 1988; Davis and Ali Choudhury 1988). They visited the homes of the families over a period of approximately 18 months, beginning weekly and gradually extending the intervals by negotiation with the parents. Once a good relationship was established it was not always necessary to continue visits with high frequency, and much easier to pick up the process and help at a crisis point. Regular supervision was provided and specialist expertise was available as necessary via the Child Development Team. Although initially funded by research money, the service was subsequently included in mainstream service budgets and has been expanded to include families of adolescents and adults with learning difficulties, as well as regular groups for Bangladeshi families.

A second service was set up in 1994, involving health visitors and community paediatricians working as parent advisers with families of pre-school children with emotional and behavioural problems (Davis, Spurr, Cox et al. 1997). They were based in two health centres in inner-city areas, and took referrals from parents themselves and from all professionals, but in practice mainly from health visitors. The procedures were very similar to those described already, except that the duration of visiting was shorter.

As a result of the success of the service (see 'Evaluation' section), it has attracted mainstream funding and has been incorporated into the tiered system described earlier. It has expanded to include more health visitors as well as staff from the early years services. In addition, we have used the model in collaboration with centres in four other European countries to set up a primary prevention project (European Early Promotion Project). This involves a public health approach, where all parents are visited by health visitors at home in the antenatal period and again at four weeks after birth. Promotional interviews, originally designed by Professors Ispanovic, Tsiantis and colleagues (Tsiantis *et al.* 1996), are conducted with the mothers as a means of helping them prepare for parenthood, and hence promoting their interaction with their children. The interviews are also the vehicle by which families whose children are at risk of psychosocial problems can be identified in the perinatal period. Those identified as in need are then visited by the health visitors weekly, using the parent adviser model in an effort to prevent difficulties arising.

Working with parents of teenagers

Although the focus of our work to date has been the pre-school period, the model is equally applicable to the teenage years, both in work directed predominantly at parents and with teenagers themselves. In principle the models of adaptation, partnership, the helping process, and the qualities and skills of facilitating the process are as appropriate in this age group as in any other, and our experience, albeit more limited, endorses the effectiveness of the approach. The emphasis upon genuine respect, which is such an important mechanism in this work with parents, cannot be overestimated in working directly with teenagers themselves, who appear more used to being instructed and controlled than listened to with empathy.

Much of our experience has come through accessing parents with younger children, but where issues related to their teenage children are included as the relationship with the parent adviser deepens. Nevertheless, we have trained school nurses who have gone on to work in specific secondary schools both with parents of teenagers and with teenagers themselves. They have tended to work with families referred by other people in the school (e.g. teachers) on a range of issues, although more informal drop-in sessions have been successfully set up in the school context.

We are currently involved in training special needs co-ordinators (SENCOs) and other teachers in schools and some of these are working with parents in secondary settings. Again, the models are the same, although the content is different. The range of issues tackled with parents varies enormously from their worries about the young peoples' anxiety and depression, fears about the influence of the peer group, drug, cigarette and alcohol use, and relationship difficulties, to behavioural problems and bereavements.

What seems salient in much of this work is the provision of a situation in which parents' concerns can be openly expressed and respected by a caring and skilled listener who encourages and facilitates the parents' own ideas and solutions. What parents frequently seem to notice is that the behaviour of the parent adviser provides them with a model of how to interact with their teenagers, listening and respecting instead of always trying to lead, control and change.

Perhaps the most elaborate application of the model so far in the teenage years has occurred through the work of Doreen Boyd and the charity Parentalk Windsor and Maidenhead (personal communication). Having trained as a parent adviser, Doreen and colleagues have developed two slightly different strands of work involving teenagers. The first was with the Thames Valley Crime Intervention Service, where, with supervision, they have been supporting parents of young offenders going through a restorative justice process. The police simply provided the parents with a telephone contact number, so that the decision to seek help and control of the process remained firmly in the parents' hands. The assumption that the parents should control all aspects of the work is crucial.

The take-up rate for the service was extremely high, and this was thought to be because of its independence from the statutory services. All parents who contacted Doreen were seen in a face-to-face meeting at least once, although most of the work was by telephone, mainly because this suited the parents. Face-to-face contacts involved one or both parents and occasionally included the teenager, at the parents' or teenager's request. The first sessions tended to last for about two hours, with subsequent contacts somewhat shorter and at weekly intervals, usually over two to three months. The usual pattern was then for the frequency of contacts to decline naturally, but with further shorter episodes of contact over the next couple of years, if necessary.

Although information sharing and occasional referral to other agencies were included, much of the work involved listening to the parents, helping them to clarify the situations confronting them, and to develop appropriate strategies. Clearly much of the content was to do with the needs and behaviour of their children, but the parents' own needs, skills, relationships and support were often at issue. Although mainly one-to-one work, some of the parents were able to join small parent groups run within the other strand of Doreen's work to help normalise their situation and to increase their social support systems. A small, unpublished follow-up study has indicated considerable success with a zero recidivism rate.

The second strand is located squarely within the voluntary sector, not the statutory youth justice system, and began respectfully as a broad consultation exercise in which Parentalk brochures were sent out asking parents what support they thought they needed. As in the parent adviser model, the emphasis was upon listening to parents and allowing them important control, as opposed to fitting them into a professionally led system. From this developed a self-referral system, driven by word of mouth and operating in a similar way to the youth justice work, with much of the contact again being by telephone. Although the frequency and duration of the contacts has tended to be shorter, it has seldom involved fewer than six sessions, with support for some parents being provided over periods of one to two years. Issues covered vary widely, but frequently include, for example, bullying, eating disorders, teenage behaviour, the effects of separation and divorce, and parental access.

Evaluation

Throughout the development of the parent adviser model, we have been trying to evaluate its effectiveness. More research is required for a definitive answer, especially in relation to adolescence, but available data in the early years of childhood indicates considerable promise. For example, three small studies suggest that trainees, as predicted, change significantly in knowledge, confidence and skills in comparison with people not taking the course (Rushton and Davis 1992; Davis et al. 1997; Lea, Clarke and Davis 1998). Systematic feedback from course participants over many years also provides clear endorsement of its value to them.

In relation to the parent adviser intervention itself, three studies have been conducted and all indicate effectiveness. Davis and Rushton (1991) evaluated the work described earlier with parents of children with severe intellectual and multiple disabilities. Consecutive referrals were allocated randomly to a parent adviser group or a group with usual services. Both were assessed before allocation and then again 15 to 21 months later. The second study was with families of children born very preterm (Avon Premature Infant Project 1998) and randomly allocated to post-hospital support as usual, a Portage worker to initiate developmental training procedures for the children via the parents at home (e.g. Daly *et al.* 1985), or a parent adviser. Thirdly, Davis and Spurr (1998) evaluated work with families of pre-school children where there were emotional or behavioural problems in the children, parenting problems or other problems in the parents. The families were assessed before intervention and four months later and compared with matched families who would have been referred if the service had existed in their neighbourhood, or were on a waiting list.

The full results are presented in the original papers and only a few examples will be given here to illustrate the effects. Measures of self-esteem were used in two of the studies, and both indicated significant benefits for the mothers in the intervention. Mothers of the children with disabilities (Davis and Rushton 1991) increased in self-esteem significantly more ($p<0.005$) than a control group, who had services as usual but not a parent adviser; the effect size was 1.21. An effect size of 0.2 is generally considered small, 0.5 is considered medium, and 0.8 or more is considered large. The same was found in the study (Davis and Spurr 1998) of mothers of pre-school children with behavioural problems ($p<0.0125$). Although the effect size was smaller (i.e. 0.38), this was probably because the intervention was much shorter.

In both studies there were other significant improvements in the mothers' psychosocial functioning. The mothers of the children with behavioural problems changed significantly more than controls on a measure of stress (the Parenting Stress Index; $p = 0.006$) and a measure of anxiety and depression (General Health Questionnaire; $p = 0.036$). The effect sizes were moderate to large (i.e. 0.56 and 0.67 respectively). In families of children with disabilities, mothers in the intervention group were significantly less stressed than the controls ($p<0.005$) at the end of the study, as measured by the Malaise Inventory (effect size: 1.15).

As a result of intervention the home environment of children with behavioural problems changed significantly more ($p<0.0125$) than in the comparison group. This was rated on the HOME Inventory, and gave a large effect size of 0.82. Intervention mothers in both studies changed significantly more in how positive they were about their children, with effect sizes of 0.40 ($p<0.05$) and 0.47 ($p<0.0125$). Mothers of children with disabilities also improved significantly more than those in the comparison group in their relationships with their husbands ($p<0.005$), with an effect size of 0.75.

The studies have also shown significant improvements in the psychosocial functioning of the children as a result of the parent adviser intervention. The behavioural problems of children with disabilities improved significantly more in the intervention condition ($p<0.005$; effect size 0.88), as did their mental age ($p<0.05$; effect size 0.32). The Avon Premature Infant Project (1998) also found significant effects on children's development progress at two years (compared to controls) for both parent advisers and parent training delivered by the Portage system (Daly *et al.* 1985). Davis and Spurr (1998) found significantly more improvement in children's behaviour for the parent adviser intervention on the Child Behaviour Checklist (Achenbach 1991) with a moderate difference in effect size of 0.5 (1.02 for intervention and 0.52 for the comparison group; $p<0.036$).

Summary and conclusions

In this chapter we have described the parent adviser model, considered the associated training and looked at the implications for service developments and support for parents of teenagers. We have also summarised the research indicating the effectiveness of the model. Help for parents of teenagers has not been easily available in the past, although this might be ameliorated if a tiered system were to operate, co-ordinating the work of all potential helpers across all agencies. Such co-ordination requires that all people working with children and families share a common purpose and understanding of the helping process. It is for this that the parent adviser model was developed with the aim of setting the helping process firmly within a partnership relationship, in which the parents' own power and self-esteem are seen as a fundamental requirement of the wellbeing of their children. The implications are that all potential helpers should be: 1) selected on the basis of their general qualities and skills for engaging parents in the process and facilitating their expertise; 2) trained appropriately in the broad psychosocial processes of helping; and 3) subsequently supervised effectively by people who also understand these processes.

The model deals with the core qualities and skills of helping and makes explicit processes that are usually taken for granted or neglected. Helping is not simply a question of giving the correct advice. Rather, it is a process of enabling parents to explore and clarify their situation sufficiently clearly to facilitate creative solutions that evolve through communication with the parents. At its most complex, however, it is a process of engaging parents, raising their self-esteem, facilitating some understanding of the problems, negotiating directions, facilitating acceptance, and empowering limited steps by way of amelioration.

Helpers require an understanding of the subtleties of these helping processes and the qualities and skills for facilitating them, and there is evidence that training and supervision are effective in improving outcomes for parents and children. Although developments and evaluative research are still required in relation to the teenage years, the parent adviser model also suggests a model of parenting teenagers that parallels the interaction between helper and parent, and can guide them both in being with teenagers. It does not, however, prevent the development of a variety of solutions to parenting problems that may be derived from other sources, including parents themselves, other helpers and alternative theories. There are few ubiquitous and guaranteed formulae, even though most helpers and parents would like to have magic wands. In both cases, the essence of the approach is an understanding of the other person (parent or teenager) and a respect for their self-determination, wisely enjoined by Gibran at the beginning.

Acknowledgments

We are grateful to the many creative and skilled helpers who have worked with us over many years and the families who have trusted us with their problems, thoughts and ideas. We should also like to acknowledge the members of the European Early Promotion Project, including Anna Paradisiotou, Stella Kyriakides, Yiannoulla Hadjipanayi and Semeli Vizacou from Cyprus, Tuula Tamminen, Kaija Puura, Merja-Maaria Turunen from Finland, Veronika Ispanovic-Radojkovic, Nenad Rudic, Jelena Radosavljev and Tijana Miladinovic from the Federal Republic of Yugoslavia, John Tsiantis, Thalia Dragonas, Effie Layiou-Lignos and Kalliroi Papadopolou from Greece, and Antony Cox and Rosemarie Roberts from the UK. We are particularly grateful to Ms Doreen Boyd for sharing her work and ideas with us and for commenting upon the manuscript. We are most grateful to the many organisations that have been involved in funding the work described here; these include the Mental Health Foundation; NHS Primary Care and Development Fund; the Gatsby Charitable Foundation; the Lambeth, Southwark and Lewisham Health Authority; the London Borough of Lewisham; the Lambeth, Southwark and Lewisham Health Action Zone; the South London and

Maudsley NHS Trust; and the Community Health South London NHS Trust.

References

Achenbach, T. (1991) *Manual for the Child Behaviour Checklist/4–18 and 1991 Profile.* Burlington, VT: University of Vermont.

Attride-Stirling, J., Davis, H., Day, C. and Sclare, I. (2000) *An Assessment of the Psychosocial Needs of Children and Families in Lewisham: Final Report.* London: South London and Maudsley NHS Trust.

Audit Commission (1999) *Children in Mind: Child and Adolescent Mental Health Services.* London: Audit Commission.

Avon Premature Infant Project (1998) 'Randomised trial of parental support for families with very preterm children.' *Archives of Disease in Childhood 79,* F4–11.

Buchan, L., Clemerson, G. and Davis, H. (1988) 'Working with families of children with special needs: The parent adviser scheme.' *Child: Care, Health and Development 14,* 81–91.

Burnard, P. (1989) *Counselling Skills for Health Professionals.* London: Chapman & Hall.

Cunningham, C. and Davis, H. (1985) *Working with Parents: Frameworks for Collaboration.* Milton Keynes: Open University Press.

Daly, B., Addington, J., Kerfoot, S. and Sigston, A. (1985) *Portage: The importance of parents.* Windsor: NFER-Nelson.

Davis, H. (1993) *Counselling Parents of Children with Chronic Illness or Disability.* Leicester: British Psychological Society Books.

Davis, H. and Ali Choudhury, P. (1988) 'Helping Bangladeshi families: Tower Hamlets Parent Adviser Scheme.' *Mental Handicap 16,* 48–51.

Davis, H., Day, C., Cox, A. and Cutler, L. (2000) 'Child and adolescent mental health needs assessment and service implications in an inner-city area.' *Clinical Child Psychology and Psychiatry 5,* 169–188.

Davis, H. and Fallowfield, L. (1991) *Counselling and Communication in Health Care.* Chichester: Wiley and Sons.

Davis, H., Kirkland, J., Jezzard, R. and Austin, C. (1998) 'The evaluation of a secondary child and adolescent mental health service.' Unpublished manuscript.

Davis, H., Cox, A., Day, C., Roberts, R., Ispanovic, V., Tsiantis, J., Layion-Ligaos, E., Purura, K., Tamminen, T., Turunen, M.M., Paradisioton, A., Hadjpanayi, Y. and Pandeli, P. (2000) *Primary Health Care Worker Training Manual.* Belgrade: Institute of Mental Health.

Davis, H. and Rushton, R. (1991) 'Counselling and supporting parents of children with developmental delay: a research evaluation.' *Journal of Mental Deficiency Research 35,* 89–112.

Davis, H. and Spurr, P. (1998) 'Parent counselling: an evaluation of a community child mental health service.' *Journal of Child Psychology and Psychiatry 39,* 365–376.

Davis, H., Spurr, P., Cox, A., Lynch, M., von Roenne, A. and Hahn, K. (1997) 'A description and evaluation of a community child mental health service.' *Clinical Child Psychology and Psychiatry 2,* 221–238.

Day, C., Davis, H. and Hind, R. (1998) 'The development of a community child and family mental health service.' *Child: Care, Health and Development 24*, 487–500.

Dickson, D., Hargie, O. and Morrow, N. (1989) *Communication Skills Training for Health Professionals*. London: Chapman & Hall.

Egan, G. (1990) *The Skilled Helper: A Systematic Approach to Effective Helping*. Pacific Grove, CA: Brooks/Cole.

Gibran, K. (1992) *The Prophet*. Harmondsworth: Penguin Books.

Kelly, G. (1955) *The Psychology of Personal Constructs*. New York: Norton.

Lea, S., Clarke, M. and Davis, H. (1998) 'Evaluation of a counselling skills course for health professionals.' *British Journal of Guidance and Counselling 26*, 159–173.

Mental Health Foundation (1999) *The Big Picture: Promoting Children and Young People's Mental Health*. London: Mental Health Foundation.

NHS Health Advisory Service (1995) *Together We Stand: A Thematic Review of Child and Adolescent Mental Health Services*. London: HMSO.

Rogers, C. (1959) 'A theory of therapy, personality and interpersonal relationships as developed in the client-centred framework.' In S. Koch (ed) *Psychology: A Study of a Science*. New York: McGraw-Hill.

Rushton, R. and Davis, H. (1992) 'An evaluation of training in basic counselling skills.' *British Journal of Guidance and Counselling 20*, 205–220.

Tsiantis, J., Dragonas, T., Cox, A. Smith, M., Ispanovic, V. and Sampaio-Faria, J. (1996) 'Promotion of children's early psychological development through primary health care services.' *Pediatric and Perinatal Epidemiology 10*, 339–354.

Chapter 8

Setting up a Parenting Teenagers Group

Dirk Uitterdijk and Jo Pitt

Introduction

This chapter aims to describe ways of setting up group-based parenting programmes for parents of teenagers. The stigma of attending a parenting course for a parent of a teenager is still extremely high. I once heard it explained that to start talking about parenting education in such a group of parents is like asking; 'How do you do sex?' We assume that we ought to know how to raise our children. After all, our parents never attended a parenting course! So why should we? We hope that we can share with you some of the strategies that can be used to work effectively with parents of adolescents. The section 'Before the group gets underway' is the longest part of this chapter. This structure reflects the importance of this part of the work: it is likely to take you the greatest amount of time if you are to run successful groups.

'Drivers slowed as police cash in' was the heading of an article in *The Times* recently (29 July 2000). The government had initiated pilot schemes in certain areas to allow police forces to plough back money received from speeding fines into policing in their own area, instead of the money going to the Treasury. The article stated that 'in one area the number of drivers trapped by the scheme had soared from 10 to 200 in a day!' Over one year the number of speeding fines increased by over 200 per cent!

Why are we mentioning this in a book on helping parents of teenagers? Because we believe that one of the main issues to be aware of when setting up and starting parenting education for parents of teenagers is to be aware of their self-interest. Why do you think the police suddenly started getting convictions for motorists who were speeding? Because the money raised would go straight back into policing in their own area. Why would they, after all, chase drivers when the money received would go to the 'anonymous' Treasury? It was in their self-interest to start fining motorists.

Over the lifetime of the three-year Lloyds TSB-funded YMCA England 403090 Parenting Teenagers project, of the 27 projects started, those most likely to succeed were the ones that kept this principle in mind. In a non-cynical way these projects were playing on parents' self-interest as a 'hook' to attract both males and females to attend their parenting project.

Before the group gets underway

Seven weekly sessions to help you become a more effective parent

starting

Tuesday March 3rd

1.30–3.30

in

St Peter's Hall

led by A. N. Other

For more information contact

Anne Other on tel: 0123 456789

The publicity leaflets have been designed, printed and distributed, the room has been prepared with a circle of chairs, the welcoming coffee is brewing – and you are waiting for the rush of parents.

It is now 1.40, one parent is standing there in embarrassment and you are beginning to suspect that there will be no others this afternoon. What do you do? Where have you gone wrong?

This scenario is not uncommon. Attracting parents to courses is not as easy as we all thought it would be when we first discovered parenting courses ourselves, and realised the enormous benefits we had reaped from them. We want to describe throughout this chapter different kinds of projects where the common aim was to run parenting courses. Whatever 'hook' is used (simple adverts, family fun days, football, theatre, school transition, social...) there are things to think about before your group even begins to get underway.

As a parenting practitioner, would you be happy when 33 parents turn up to your parenting course, many of whom are couples? Many leaders would be happy with five or six parents turning up.

Let me tell you what happened on one occasion when a family fun day took place in a sports centre. Wouldn't it be in the interest of parents to offer them activities where they can attend as a family unit? We are all aware of the demise of the 'OXO cube' family. Many of us don't regularly eat together at the meal-table anymore, particularly in dual-working families.

I was due to attend this family fun day and say a few words about the reasons for attending a parenting course. On the Monday I phoned them to ask how many people had signed up: only 25 at that point... I seriously wondered whether it would be worth the five-hour journey to make a five-minute speech. We did go, as a family, and were, together with the staff, amazed at over 250 parents and children attending! They could enjoy wall climbing, trampolining, line dancing, arts and crafts, 'dads and lads' football, badminton and many other activities. Food was offered and I gave my little speech. The parents and the children were invited to attend a parenting course a month later using the 'Parentalk' videos and materials. Thirty-three parents and forty children turned up on this Saturday evening. They were treated to a basket of food, after which the children attended sporting activities in the sports hall. The parents watched the Parentalk video on a big screen and divided into smaller groups during discussion time. Because the children were cared for, many couples took part in the course. Further family fun days have been planned at other venues across the country.

'Who are you? – Why are you doing this work? – Who funds you? – Who is the course aimed at?'

These ought to be the first questions that anyone considering joining a parenting programme should ask. Those running them should also be clear about their answers to these questions and the implications of their answers. Parenting courses are now offered by people working for many government agencies, often targeting particular groups of parents, and also by the voluntary sector and the churches. Each will have their own agenda.

For example, **health visitors** often run courses. They have a natural access to parents in the first crucial years and can see all the advantages of bringing parents together to share experiences and develop friendships, as well as the more obvious ones of imparting some parenting skills. There are potential problems, however. A health visitor has an ongoing professional relationship with her clients, but as a facilitator she is likely to draw on her personal experiences, to join the group as an equal parent. It is important to do so if the group is to be an empowering one based on recognition of parents' strengths. But it may alter the way her clients see her afterwards; it may in some way lead to an altered professional relationship. If she has personally invited clients to join her group, those who choose not to come may feel they have let her down, and might not afterwards feel so easy in the one-to-one relationship that is the foundation of her work.

Teachers also see a need for courses. They can see how their work might be enhanced if they could share their approaches to children with the parents. They have their own agenda, wanting perhaps consistent behaviour and an excellent learning environment both at home and at school. They might wish to run a parenting course themselves – but are fearful about how parents might feel about sharing openly with their child's teacher. As facilitators of a parenting group they will not be the authority figures who hold the knowledge, but equals. Once again, if they share openly with the group, their professional relationship with parents may be altered. The school may pay or persuade someone else to offer courses to parents, or may even offer training to parents to do this. Again, it is important to see things from the parents' perspective – how might they feel about a fellow-parent leading a course, and how might the facilitator parent feel about putting themselves up as 'the perfect parent' among their peers? How might their children feel?

Adult/community education is another area where parenting courses are to be found. With imaginative marketing it would appear that this is a natural home for this kind of work. Care must be taken over the venue if the course is to be attractive to all kinds of parents. It must not be too reminiscent of a classroom – the coffee bar area may sometimes be more appropriate than the classroom.

Youth Offending Teams running parenting courses will also have their own agenda. They will need to think carefully whether to place parents receiving Parenting Orders into a group of 'ordinary' parents who have chosen to attend, or to run courses specially for 'their' parents. In the former case these parents could be absorbed into the group, might find friendship and support, and could realise that their problems are not so very different from those of other parents. In either case there is likely to be some anger at being made to come, and this will need to be accepted and understood before any useful work can take place within the group.

Courses are run by organisations within the **voluntary sector** or by **churches**. Often there is someone with a passion about this work and they have sought hard for funding to do it. They believe strongly that the voluntary sector is an appropriate and non-threatening home for such work. They will still need to be able to answer the questions 'Who are you? Why are you doing this work?' They may also have to justify their qualifications and training. If courses are held by church organisations or in church buildings, or even have a proportion of church funding, there will always be some suspicion about the content and the underlying aims.

Groups may also be run by **social services**, in **family centres**, as part of one of the **government initiatives** like Health Action Zones, Sure Start, On Track and so on. Each organisation will thus have its own agenda and its own source of funding. This can lead to a piecemeal approach to parenting work in an area, and it can be difficult for parents, let alone professionals, to find out 'what is happening' locally. Many areas are forming local parenting forums, which aim to bring together all those working in this field, as well as parents, to share information, experience and good practice and present a cohesive parenting support service. There are many examples of such forums around the country, and each is likely to be different. Information and advice about them can be obtained from the Parenting Education and Support Forum Regional Development Officers.

Materials

Not only will an organisation target a particular group of parents largely because of how they are funded; they will also need to choose a programme or materials that will suit their proposed group. Choosing the right materials is a prime concern of the leaders of parenting courses. Our advice is to use courses where all the planning has been done for you, if you are new to this group work. Family Caring Trust courses (see Useful Addresses) are designed for use by ordinary parents and are the most widely used materials in the UK at present. When you are more experienced you can be more creative, using course materials from several different organisations and using a 'pick and mix' approach. Many groups use Positive Parenting courses 'Time out for parents', or the Parentalk course, originally developed by Care for the Family, but now marketed by the Parentalk charity, used by over 1700 groups nationally. A ten-session DAD course for fathers was written by Care for the Family in conjunction with the YMCA Dads and Lads project. 'Let's Talk Parenting' (Sue Millar and Joe Ward) is another course especially useful for those working with parents of children causing concern at school and more generally. Many Youth Offending Teams use these materials. Some courses require a good level of reading skill; others work from cartoons and very few words. There are, in fact, so many courses to choose from that if a newcomer to the field were to see a display of the materials available, it would be difficult to know which to choose. The Parenting Education and Support Forum has available on request a number of 'Practitioner Reviews' of courses. It is also important to network and exchange experiences with other facilitators. Once the group has started, the materials chosen may still need to be adapted as the course develops.

Attracting parents to courses

One of the principles of community development work is to start where people are at, to work from the bottom up. It is useful, when designing publicity, or when thinking about offering courses, to start with yourself – would you put yourself forward for a course? Possibly not, if it were offered in a note from the school – you might feel that such courses were for 'those others' but not for you. Why not? Only rather odd people, or people who have a real need (i.e. their children are a real problem) would be there, and you do not wish to be seen as one of those. You might, however, be persuaded to try it if someone you respected or liked personally invited you, but you would need some reassurance. You might want to know who was going to run the course, and also why they were running it. So how can you expect parents to come on receipt of a note from school? We should not expect people to do things that we ourselves would not do.

Another principle is to start with small, very achievable plans – success breeds success and creates optimism. This will help to ensure that a parenting course is really rooted in a local community. If it aims to attract a total of only ten parents, it is more successful if ten come from a total of thirty invited, than ten out of a whole school of a thousand. It is a good idea to give a talk *about* parenting courses to groups, and give a twenty-minute sample of a course, as this will dispel much of the misunderstanding about what such courses are really about. When people realise how full of common sense they are, how the things you might discuss are the very ordinary things like getting a sullen teenager to do his share of the washing-up, they are engaged. They start asking how they can enrol, and a series of sessions can be offered. This would be the time to discuss days and times and venues – the days and times that would suit the potential parents, not necessarily the ones that suit the facilitator. Regarding venue, local parents will soon let you know which are acceptable places for them to meet, and which are not. If possible it is better to be guided by their ideas on this than to presume a greater knowledge of their area and community.

Which might be the groups that want to hear about parenting courses? Any group that already meets regularly – a church group, a club or association, a PTA, a parents and toddlers group, a family centre group, a literacy group – could be persuaded to invite a speaker. School heads can be persuaded to allow a talk at parents' assembly at an appropriate time of year (e.g. Mothering Sunday, Father's Day).

A large, international group of parent effectiveness training co-ordinators was asked what were their best and worst marketing strategies when trying to attract parents onto courses (Pitt, J., 1999).

Their best strategies were:

word of mouth and personal contact	38 per cent
running successful programmes	19 per cent
giving demonstrations, e.g. at PTA meetings	11 per cent
leaving contact name in all books, materials, etc.	8 per cent
co-operation with other bodies	8 per cent
making it free	8 per cent
one-day conferences	4 per cent
TV appearances	4 per cent

and their worst strategies, and other factors leading to poor attendance:

adverts in magazines, journals, newspapers	45 per cent
mailing alone	25 per cent
contacting organisations without personal contact	10 per cent
'just waiting'	5 per cent
poor quality instructors	5 per cent
unsatisfactory results from course from participants	5 per cent
engaging a professional media company	5 per cent

'Word of mouth' – the personal touch – is clearly important, but there can be no word of mouth before the start of your first course. How do you try to introduce a course to parents for the very first time in an area? It helps if there has been some good local or national media coverage – the right sort of story in a local newspaper about some very ordinary parents who have tried and enjoyed a course. (Local journalists often interpret the message in an insensitive way: e.g. 'Help now available for parents in trouble.' It is important to ask to see the finished copy before it goes to print.)

A good way to get started is to invite several people to help you test out a new course – they feel flattered at being invited and are keen to join. 'Have you thought about doing a parenting course?' or 'Why don't you try a parenting course?' can invoke feelings of guilt and shame at having been found wanting in their parenting skills. If some of those invited are health visitors, social workers or teachers, this can be the first stage in overcoming local professional suspicion about what you are trying to offer. It can also lead to some referrals. For an agency to refer parents on to a parenting course requires a level of knowledge about the course and a level of trust in the facilitators.

The second best strategy from the list above is not surprising – 'running successful programmes'. A good reputation is vital and a poor one most damaging. Your reputation needs to be earned and this can take some time. Another strategy that can work well when you are more established is to send details of a proposed course to participants who have been on a previous one with a friendly note: 'If you enjoyed your course, please tell a friend about this next one.' Parents often say that their friends are intrigued to hear about the strange course they are going on, and will ask them for details as the course progresses. There are always those who take up a new idea at the first opportunity, and those who wait until they feel very sure, and have seen the evidence of its merits in their friends.

Once they have overcome the barriers to attending the first session, parents do not usually need further persuading. It is, of course, important to be sensitive to parents' commitments, for example, half-terms and school meetings. A willingness and ability to be reasonable and flexible is appreciated.

The following hints from adult education may also help when thinking about marketing parenting courses. These elements are seen as vital:

- friendliness and approachability of teachers
- non-judgemental approach
- enjoyment – fun
- potential to improve career prospects
- not just for brainy people.

A key finding in the evaluation by the Trust for the Study of Adolescence of the three-year YMCA England 403090 Parenting Education and Support Project is the importance of using a 'hook' to attract parents to your parenting courses.

> Talking to the staff I became aware of the enormous amount of youngsters playing sport at Plymouth YMCA (400 boys between the ages of 8 and 14 every week). I asked whether it would be an idea to invite the dads to play sport alongside their sons. Mark Peard, then programme director, started the first official Dads and Lads initiative in February 1998. We were able to give them a small starter grant of £331. Eleven dads and fourteen lads came along to the first session. Not bad considering the session was held on a Saturday evening! You try and get a group of men together at any time of the week!

> After several months a special evening was planned in conjunction with the start of the World Cup. 'Why not get these dads and lads together, offer them some food and then while the lads are playing sport have a short session with the dads about what it is like to be a father?' This was to be the start of a special 'father course' using the 60-minute father material written by Rob Parsons of Care for the Family.

Golden opportunities for intervention

Children are not the only ones for whom key stages are important. There are key stages in a parent's life when they are more likely to think seriously about a parenting course. Times of transition and times of stress are moments when it is a good idea to offer help. Thus a good time to offer an initial course for parents of teenagers is when children transfer from primary school to secondary school, and parents are starting to think about the rumours they have heard about teenagers and problems. Parents are more easily persuaded to come to a course at the familiar primary school while their child is in the top year, than to the more forbidding secondary school. Even a very shortened course, or an introduction to parenting courses as part of the preparation for transition, can alert them to the fact that help will be at hand later if they should want it. Then, when the problems start to seem insurmountable and parents feel isolated and even ashamed at their children's behaviour, they might remember, when invited to a parenting course, that it might be something that would help. There is an impression around that they 'might be found out, found to be wanting' if they participate in one of 'those groups.' Thus a gentle introduction of the idea needs to be around while things are going well, and there is no guilt or shame felt (at the time of transition), before the actual course is offered at the time of stress, the moment of need.

The stigma of admitting in front of your friends that you may possibly be experiencing problems with your teenagers is very great. Would it, therefore, be in the interest of parents if we gave them the anonymous opportunity to watch a play about parents' and teenagers' issues? Would we take away much of the stigma that way? After all, it should be easier to watch a play about these issues than to participate in a group, where you are required to lift the curtain of parenting privacy.

> 'One of the most exciting ways of conveying information!' Y-Touring commissioned Judith Johnson to write 'Double the Trouble', a contemporary comedy about being a parent, being a teenager and being a family. We received funding from the Home Office to fund the national tour of this play, which took place between February and April 2001 and will take place again sometime in 2002. The vision is to reach 6000 parents over two six-week periods, with up to two performances per day. We can offer the play free to any voluntary organisation. We also hope that the play will be a catalyst for further parenting education. It's easier to

invite a parent once they've been in your building than to invite them 'cold' to a 'parenting teenagers' course. 'Double the Trouble' – a new comedy for parents. Because it is not always funny being a teenager. Or as one commentator aptly suggested: 'Solving a crisis with a drama'.

How far would you go for your child's education? It was the Right Honourable Jack Straw, MP, who said at a Barnardos 'Parenting Matters' conference on May 25 1999: 'I can remember like yesterday the day I entered secondary school. The other children seemed huge!' For many of us the transition from primary to secondary school brings back lots of memories. Unfortunately, far too often they are negative.

Nowadays parents are offered a choice of which secondary school their child will attend. They need to fill in forms, which have to be sent to the school by mid-January. Schools at the top of league tables are often heavily oversubscribed. Parents go as far as feigning separation, renting properties in the catchment area or nominally following a religion, in order to ensure that their child attends the school of their choice. Parenting experts talk about 'golden opportunities of intervention' in the life of parents and children. If parents are willing to go this far for their children, isn't this one of those moments? Wouldn't it be in the interest of parents to attend an evening in the primary school before this school selection date has passed (which would mean before Christmas) to find out more about which school to choose? Several schools successfully experimented with running 'Moving on' or transition evenings. Needless to say, they were very well attended!

> We invited both the parent and the Year 6 child to come to the school. We made extensive use of nostalgia, playing the music of the era when the parents were teenagers themselves. It's not a bad thing for a parent to remember what it was like for them when they went through adolescence themselves!

> We did a quiz aimed at both the parents and the children. In that way they could laugh at each other! (Did you/ do you really like that music, those clothes, that hairstyle?) During the introduction to the transition evening in Wallasey one employee, unbeknown to the other, put a photo on the overhead projector, taken during the time when the other employee was a teenager! The problem was: great minds think alike! The tables were turned and a photo was displayed of the other worker with long hair and decidedly dodgy clothes!

We invited secondary school teachers to give a five-minute commercial on their school. Parents could ask questions and, while this was going on, the children were in another room talking about what scared them most about the transition. Finally, we offered the option of attending a parenting course on teenage issues the following week. Would you be more inclined to attend a parenting course introduced in this way rather than if you received a flyer from your child? (Or to be more truthful: after you find the flyer at the bottom of their schoolbag!) One parent wrote: 'An excellent evening to introduce children to secondary school, even thinking back to the time when I went through this.' Could these evenings even become statutory, as part of what schools are required to offer to the parents during this important time?

Parents have said that they would not go on a course provided by their child's school because they feared the lynch mob, or because they didn't want to talk about their child's problems in front of people they might meet at school functions or in the street. They are concerned about the privacy of their children, concerned, in short, about the ability of the group to maintain confidentiality. They would, however, go to a different area, because they recognised their need. Other parents would only go if the course were in their immediate neighbourhood – travel problems, problems of time, wanting to belong even more to a local community... There is a case for having both kinds of courses on offer. We need to accept that parents want to be able to choose whatever is most comfortable for them.

Leadership skills

There is much to think about here but, as a broad principle, the more likely there are to be real problems within a group, the better trained the group facilitator needs to be. An ideal situation would be co-leadership, one male and one female facilitator. The advantages of using well-trained 'amateurs' – other parents – are great. It gives a clear message that there is not a 'right' way (ours) and a 'wrong' way (yours) to bring up children and teenagers. The course is more about discussion, sharing, trying out (and then maybe discarding) alternative ways of doing things, and about finding out that you are not alone in your troubles. These are the things that parents tell us time and again are beneficial about joining a group. Some groups, such as those with some or all parents attending because of a Parenting Order, may need a facilitator with much experience. There may be antagonism and even fury about being there, and if this is not dealt with, shared and accepted in the very beginning, the group is likely to fail. Handling issues like these is not for the untrained and inexperienced.

The training that might be needed for people to undertake this kind of work is too complex and too important an issue to discuss here, and is addressed in more detail in a later chapter. The importance of a potential leader having themselves 'been on' a parenting course cannot be stressed enough. This will encourage reflection (what it felt like for me) and empathy (what it might feel like for you). Some understanding of how adults learn and what might motivate them, and also of how groups function, is also important.

A leader is likely at some stage to touch upon an issue that is very disturbing for a parent, leading to tears or an inexplicable outbreak of anger or any other uncontrolled or even uncontrollable behaviour. If the leader is on their own it can be difficult to deal with this kind of situation. It is a good idea to stress early on in a course that these groups are *not* therapy groups, just friendly, chatty sessions sharing ideas and tips on raising children. If they are discussing an issue in pairs, it is wise to suggest they do not choose something too deep or troublesome. If the parents find that something on the course starts to trouble them, it may be a sign that further help is needed. A file of telephone numbers for more specialist advice or counselling that they can ask to borrow is essential.

The support needed for group leaders is also addressed elsewhere. Expensive though it may seem, having two workers will ensure that there is a proper debriefing after each session and the next session is properly prepared. Discussion needs to take place after each session to ensure that the needs of all those in the group are being met. If a particular course is being followed, it needs to be used flexibly enough to meet these needs. Each group will be different.

The group

No one should be expected to join a group where they find they are the only one who is male, or single, or black, or the only couple, or there under duress, or anything else that might cause a member to feel awkward. Such a situation might be avoided if plenty of information is exchanged at the time of enquiry or booking. A home visit is useful and can encourage a shy person to come – they will know that they will now recognise at least one of the people there, and have the advantage that they already have a relationship with one of the leaders. Few people find it easy to join a group – let alone one where you might be expected to share what might be really intimate details of your life.

Groups are not appropriate for everybody – parents must be allowed the dignity of choice. They may not be appropriate for parents who are in the middle of a crisis, as giving out and listening is as important a part of parenting groups as telling and taking in. A parent in a crisis might have too great a need to listen to others, and might find others' problems trivial. They might make things even worse for themselves by antagonising others in the group, leaving themselves even more isolated and rejected than before. A parent in a crisis probably needs individual sessions.

Groups of eight to ten seem to work well – there is enough experience in a group of that size to give all a chance to participate, without putting too much onus on anyone to play a large part. Groups of five or six can become too intimate; groups of twelve and above can spoil the intimacy and might need to break up into smaller groups too frequently.

Some courses for parents are accredited and will therefore enable a participant to receive credits and a certificate of achievement. Other courses are not accredited but include in the 'package' some certificates of attendance that can be given out. Some parents like to receive such a certificate, others find them patronising. It is important that we do not make parents feel that because they have attended a course and received a certificate, they are now 'perfect' parents. But more important, we do not want them to feel that every time they revert to their old ways, they are somehow not worthy of this certificate. They will not be expected to achieve perfection all the time.

Conclusion

More time is likely to be spent thinking about and preparing for a first parenting course than actually running it. Working together with other local agencies will ensure that parents know where to find information about parenting courses. It will also help to encourage a spirit of collaboration rather than competition among agencies. The importance of using a 'hook' to attract parents and spending some time appreciating where they are coming from cannot be underestimated.

It is worth remembering that, as Gillian Pugh once said at a Parenting Education and Support Forum conference: 'Families will not walk through a door that says: "Failure".'

Further reading

Neville, D., King, L. and Benk, D. (1988) Promoting Positive Parenting of Teenagers. Aldershot: Arena.

Parenting Education and Support Forum Guidelines (see 'Useful Addresses')

References

Pitt, J. (1999) 'Marketing' in Churchill Fellowship Report: Promoting Parenting Skills 1999 (Available from J. Pitt, Witherholme farm, Whemby, York YO61 4SF)

Times, the (2000) 'Drivers slowed as police cash in' 29 July.

Chapter 9

Schools as a Context for Working with Parents

The 'Living with Teenagers... Supporting Parents' Project

Debi Roker and Helen Richardson

This chapter describes and evaluates an intervention which explored different ways of offering advice and support to the parents of teenagers. The project was undertaken in collaboration with a state secondary school over the course of a school year. The chapter describes the background to the project, the research undertaken into the needs of parents, the types of support offered, and the results of the intervention. Finally, a number of key learning points are identified and a number of general conclusions drawn.

Background to the project: schools as a context for parent education and support

Each of the chapters in this book has highlighted the public and policy issues raised by strategies to support the parents of teenagers. All the chapters have reflected on the fact that there is much more information and support available for parents of young children, despite the new and difficult issues that are faced by the parents of young people (Coleman 1997).

As the chapters have also made clear, however, a wide variety of strategies are now being explored to offer information, advice and support to the parents of young people. Outside of the school context, these include group-based parenting courses run by statutory and voluntary bodies (see

Roker and Coleman 1998, for a review), telephone helplines (such as ParentLine), and materials in the form of books, audio-tapes and videos. Within the school context, support for parents is variable and patchy, with information and support for parents most commonly offered through group-based courses, parents' evenings, one-off talks, and support from in-dividual teachers during a crisis or particular difficulty.

We believe that the school context offers a valuable setting in which to offer support to a large number of parents. During the mid-1990s, the Trust for the Study of Adolescence (TSA) was actively seeking ways of working with schools to offer support to parents of teenagers. It was at this time that TSA was approached by Kent Social Services (KSS), who were in-terested in undertaking an innovative school-based project. Like TSA, KSS was convinced that offering parents of teenagers support could provide both short-term and long-term benefits, in particular reducing the need for social services intervention in the future. Both organisations believed that a universal rather than a targeted approach would be most valuable, and would enable support to be offered to the broadest range of parents. It was agreed to offer this support in a school context, in order to ensure that in-formation and support was offered to a wide range of parents.

Reflecting this approach, a number of principles were agreed between TSA and KSS, that formed the basis of a school-based intervention to support the parents of teenagers. These principles were:

- parents of teenagers and pre-teenagers have a right to information, advice and support in relation to bringing up their children

- the provision of such support can have a range of positive outcomes, including better parent–teenager relationships and a reduction in risk behaviours among young people

- such support should be offered on a universal basis, thus avoiding the targeting and stigmatising of individual parents or families

- the support offered must be appropriate and responsive to parents' individual needs, circumstances and culture, as well as building upon the strengths within families and in their relationships

- early support for parents, particularly those in disadvantaged communities, can prevent difficulties and possible statutory intervention later on

- any intervention that is offered should be fully evaluated in order to identify outcomes, good practice and lessons for future work.

With these key principles in mind, TSA agreed to undertake a school-based intervention and evaluation, funded by KSS and with additional funding from the Carnegie Trust. The aim was to offer a three-stage intervention, as follows:

- Stage 1: initial research with parents to explore their current relationship with their children, their information and support needs, and the form in which they would like support

- Stage 2: provision of support services based on the views of parents

- Stage 3: a final phase of research to explore parents' use of and views about the support provided, and ways of improving such work in the future.

The school involved in the intervention, and the design of the fieldwork, are described below.

Fieldings School

The school involved ('Fieldings School') had long requested additional support for its parents, and was keen to participate in the project when approached by KSS. The school catered for 11–16-year-olds, and was in the centre of a medium-sized town in Kent. Located in an area of economic and social disadvantage, there were high rates of unemployment and crime locally, and large estates of poor quality housing. The school had a large number of pupils with special educational needs, and a high level of exclusions and pupil turnover.

Following discussions with the school, it was agreed to work only with Year 8 parents (i.e. parents of 12–13-year-olds). The parents in this year group were turning to the school for information and advice in relation to their teenagers, in numbers that were stretching the time and expertise of school staff. Further, the nature of the project (described below) meant that the costs of offering the project to the whole school would have been prohibitive. Following discussions between TSA, KSS and the senior staff team at the school, it was agreed to undertake the project as described below.

Research with parents and young people: Time 1

All Year 8 parents were contacted at the start of the intervention, to explain the nature of the project and the services that could be made available within it. An official 'launch' of the project was also held at the school. All parents were asked, at this stage, if they would be individually interviewed. Where there were two parents in the home, both were approached for interview. The interview schedule used was semi-structured, and lasted 1–2.5 hours. The following question areas were included:

- demographic and descriptive items, including number of children and/or stepchildren, parents' employment, and whether they had a partner

- relationships with their child, including whether it was easier or more difficult to be their parent now that they were older, and the ways in which their child had changed in the last few years

- difficult issues or areas of disagreement with their son or daughter, and any concerns they had about the young person

- how much information and support they had in relation to the teenage years, and whether they would like more information and/or support

- what they felt they did well as a parent, and what they were proud of in their children

- the form in which they would like information and support provided within the project.

The interview also contained a self-completion questionnaire, which included statements about the relationship with the Year 8 child, and questions about knowledge and support in relation to parenting. These questions were coded on a 1–10 scale.

In addition to collecting information through individual interviews with parents, analyses were also undertaken of the school's records. Two measures were derived from the information collected about pupil behaviour, contact with parents, and pupil events. These were a measure of contact between the school and the home, as a result of difficulty with the child's progress or behaviour, and a measure of disruptive or difficult child events during the course of the year, recorded by teachers, and which did not involve contacting parents. Both these measures were coded as a low, medium or high number of events.

The young people in the year group also completed a questionnaire, with several of the items matching those in the parents' questionnaire and interview schedule. In total, 70 questionnaires were completed by the young people.

The year group consisted of 167 individual parents from 99 families. Of this group 102 parents from 66 families were interviewed. The interviews were undertaken from December 1997 to February 1998. Of those interviewed, 21 per cent of the families had no income earners, 22 per cent were single-parent families, and 62 per cent of those who worked were in skilled manual and manual occupations.

The data for the first round of interviews (Time 1) showed a variety of views and issues being faced by parents, and varying degrees of support currently available to them. Of this group, 52 per cent thought that it was harder to be the parent of the Year 8 child now that they were older. The majority of arguments and disagreements with the young people concerned household activities, pocket money/income, and the time they went to bed. Approximately 20 per cent of the families were experiencing considerable difficulties or conflict in the family, with the young people concerned involved in crime or drug use, or in the process of being excluded from school. Sources of support for parents were most commonly named as parents and grandparents; however, 25 per cent of those interviewed said that they had no source of support in relation to bringing up teenagers. The majority of the parents interviewed were very positive about the project, feeling that there were few sources of information and support available for the parents of teenagers.

There were also significant differences between the views of the parents and the young people on a number of areas. These results showed that the parents believed they had more influence over their teenagers than the teenagers themselves believed. This included influence over the time the young people went to bed, their use of alcohol, their use of illegal drugs, and whether they got involved in crime. Also, the parents were less positive than the young people about the influence of friends and the peer group, and had greater confidence that they knew where the young people were when they were out of the house. These results showed that many parents underestimated the amount of smoking, drinking and vandalism that their children were involved in.

Following analysis of the Time 1 interview data, three main types of information and support were identified. The parents most commonly wanted the following types of services:

1. materials and information about adolescent development and particular issues, which they could use at home

2. meeting with other parents to discuss issues and share information and ideas

3. having one person available to them for one-to-one help and support.

The provision of services at the school was designed around the needs identified by the parents in the interviews. These are outlined below.

Service provision

The three services were provided over the course of a school year during 1997/98. They were made available as follows:

1. *Materials about adolescence:* Parents were offered any three of the following materials, free of charge and for them to keep – one video (*Living With Teenagers*), two books (*Teenagers in the Family* and *Teenagers and Sexuality*), and eight audio-tapes and booklets on topics including sexuality, drugs, divorce, alcohol, families, suicide and self-harm, stress and step-families.

2. *Group-based parenting programmes:* Two courses were offered, one in the daytime and one in the evening. These were eight weeks long (two hours per session), and were run by experienced facilitators from a national parenting organisation. The courses addressed issues such as communication, conflict, negotiation, focusing on positive behaviour, the needs of parents, and difficult issues.

3. *One-to-one support:* A parent adviser was appointed to provide one-to-one information and support to the parents in the year group. The experienced counsellor and family worker appointed to this role was available to parents for one day a week at the school (no appointment needed), from 10am to 5pm, and also in the evening over the telephone, from 7pm to 9pm.

All three of the services were free, and parents could choose to use one, two or all three of them.

Research with parents and young people: Time 2

At the end of the project (summer 1998), all the Year 8 parents were approached again for an interview. By this time some 15 families had left the school, either because of the relocation of the parent, or the pupil being excluded or transferred from the school. The same interview schedule was used to allow for comparison between the Time 1 and Time 2 data, with additional questions included to ask parents about their use of, and views about, the services offered in the project. Similarly, the young people also completed another questionnaire. In total at Time 2, 80 individual parents were interviewed. Of those interviewed at the two time points, 61 parents had data at both Time 1 and Time 2.

Use of the services

In total, 70 per cent of the families used at least one of the services. Of this group, 40 per cent used one service, 23 per cent used two, and 7 per cent used all three. Information about the use of each of the services is given below, including where appropriate the views of the facilitators providing the service.

1. *Materials:* Thirty-five families (35% of the total) ordered a total of 111 materials. The most frequently ordered materials were the Carlton *Living with Teenagers* video (ordered by 31 families), and the *Teenagers in the Family* book (ordered by 20 families).

2. *Parenting courses:* Twelve parents attended two 'Living with Teenagers' courses, comprising six individuals and three couples. There were five parents on the daytime course, and seven parents on the evening one; there were nine women and three men. The evaluations completed by the parents were generally positive, but mixed. Several parents commented on how the course was very difficult at the start, and had not included what they had been expecting. However, most added that they had learnt a lot of very valuable things in relation to being the parent of a teenager. A few parents commented that their issues were so serious or complex that the course could not really have helped them in any substantial way.

   Interviews were undertaken with the facilitators following completion of the two courses. Both of the facilitators described the courses as 'very difficult'. Despite a detailed flyer explaining the course ethos and methods, many parents were not expecting the courses to be run in the way that they were. Most clearly expected a lecture-style format, with information and tips on young people and drugs, or the law. The first few sessions were therefore largely spent introducing the parents to the more experiential style of the courses, and demonstrating the value of exploring such things as communication styles, negotiation, and language.

Reflecting on the courses overall, both tutors described a 'huge sense of disempowerment' among the parents. Many parents were clearly very desperate for help and support, and felt overwhelmed by things that were happening to them at the time (in their lives generally, such as unemployment, or in relation to their children, such as a poor relationship with their teenager). However, the parents often found it difficult to relate the sorts of things addressed on the course to their own lives, and to believe that there was any way to address their problems. Many parents were despairing and feeling a great sense of hopelessness.

It is of note that both facilitators believed that by about week 5, the parents had come to trust them and felt more able to open up and discuss their views and feelings. Indeed, several of the parents commented on how they had begun to 'get into' the course, and could see how it might make a difference to them and their relationships. As one of the facilitators commented, 'the course ended just as they had learnt how to get something from it'.

3. *Parent adviser.* The parent adviser had a very small number of contacts with parents in her first two months in the school. On average one parent a week visited or telephoned, often in relation to something that they needed help with, but that was not directly related to their Year 8 child. One single mother with reading difficulties, for example, asked for help to complete a form. The adviser also saw a teacher from the school who asked to see her, and a few parents from another year group who had heard that she was available.

In total, nine Year 8 parents had a total of 13 contacts with the parent adviser during the first two months of the project. As a result of the low level of contacts made, a meeting was held between the parent adviser, TSA and senior staff at the school. A number of strategies were discussed, in particular ways in which more parents could be enabled to utilise the service. It was argued by the school's staff that the service was not being offered in a way that was consistent with their usual mode of working with parents. Thus parents at the school were 'managed' more, and did not expect to have to be pro-active about accessing school-based services. Further, a great deal of contact with parents, although initiated by letter, was most commonly undertaken by phone.

The school's staff therefore suggested that the parent adviser should individually telephone all the Year 8 families involved in the project to remind them that she was there, and to discuss any issues if they wished to. The TSA team had reservations about this suggestion, feeling that parents might find it intrusive. However, it was agreed that the adviser should start telephoning round the parents, and see how this strategy was received. She started telephoning at the end of April 1998, and the process continued intermittently (between contacts with parents) through to June.

By the end of the project in July 1998 the parent adviser had had contact with 62 of the 99 families (63% of all families). Following all contacts with parents, a record sheet was completed. This showed that, of those parents contacted:

- 40 of the parents had a 'brief' conversation with the adviser. These parents said that they were not experiencing any difficulties at that time, but almost all added that they appreciated that the adviser had called them, and that they felt pleased and reassured that someone was taking an interest in them.

- 22 had 'long' conversations, often involving follow-up contacts, which included talking through issues raised, counselling and giving advice or making referrals

- 37 of the parents were not contactable, or their children had left the school.

The parent adviser commented at the end of this process that '99 per cent really appreciated the call, were really pleased that I'd phoned...felt someone was taking an interest and was there if they needed them'.

In the general interview undertaken with the parent adviser at the end of the project, her view was that the majority of parents were 'very positive' about the parent adviser service. Many parents had commented to her on how difficult it was to get information about issues arising in the teenage years, and/or that it was good to find someone who was able to listen and discuss things with them 'without constantly looking at their watches'. Indeed, the vast majority of parents that she spoke to weren't looking for a specific solution to a problem. As she described it:

> [they] just needed to talk to someone, to look at ways for them to cope. They didn't want...or need solutions as such, they just wanted to talk to someone about what was happening, their child's moodiness, the tempers that teenagers can have, how useless they can make you feel, that sort of thing.

An analysis of the parent adviser records showed that parents brought two types of issues to the adviser services. Approximately 50 per cent of the issues were school-related, including such things as disruption in class, bullying, violence and special needs. In relation to special needs, she added, there was a clear sense of not knowing what help was available, feeling 'lost' in complex diagnoses and concepts, and feeling unsupported. The remaining 50 per cent of issues raised were home-related. These included, in particular, difficult or conflictual relationships, problems with step-families, and poor relationships with siblings.

Finally, it is of note that the parent adviser did not only see Year 8 parents during her time at the school. She also saw teachers, young people, and parents from other year groups. This was, she felt, a very valuable extension of her role, and one that she believed gave the school as a whole some 'ownership' over her role. This is an important consideration in future work.

The following section describes the parents' views of the services provided in the project, and the results of the longitudinal evaluation.

Parents' views of the project and comparison of Time 1 and Time 2 results

In a project such as this, a key outcome is the use that the parents make of the services. This information was given above. It was also clearly important to explore the parents' views about the project, and to identify any changes in the key measures between the Time 1 and Time 2 interviews. These results are given here.

In general, the vast majority of the parents were extremely positive about the project. At Time 2, 90 per cent of those who were interviewed described the project as 'excellent' or 'very good'. This view was expressed regardless of whether or not the parent used any of the services. The main reason given for this was that it was reassuring to know that help and support were available if parents needed them.

Comparisons of the data from Time 1 and Time 2 showed that there were improvements in parents' information, understanding, and the level of support they felt they had in relation to bringing up teenagers. Crucially, there was a greater proportion of parents at Time 2 than at Time 1 who said that they had 'no major worries or concerns' about their teenager, rising from 19 per cent at Time 1 to 40 per cent at Time 2. There was also a one-third reduction in the numbers who said that they had 'no sources' of support between Time 1 and Time 2, from 24 per cent to 16 per cent. Finally, those parents who said that they felt that they knew enough about the changes of the teenage years rose from 64 per cent at Time 1 to 82 per cent at Time 2.

There were also some significant changes between Time 1 and Time 2 in the scale items which were incorporated into the interviews. These results showed that parents felt more knowledgeable and supported at the end of the project. Thus there were increased mean scores which showed that at Time 2, compared with Time 1:

- fewer parents wanted to significantly change their relationship with their teenager

- more parents felt that they communicated well with their teenager

- more parents felt they had a good degree of knowledge about the changes of the teenage years.

It is of note also that some significant differences were found between those parents who used the services and those who did not. Those parents with high and medium level contact with the school during the course of the year (in relation to problems with their child's progress or behaviour) were more likely to use the services. In total, 67 per cent of these families used at least one of the services. A similar pattern was found for the measure of disruptive or difficult child events during the course of the year. Those parents with the highest number of events were less likely to use the materials, or to attend a parenting course, but were more likely to have contact with the parent adviser.

A range of results has been presented in this chapter so far. The remainder of the chapter details the learning points from the project.

Learning points from the project

The intervention described above aimed to offer information, advice and support to the parents of teenagers. A number of learning points arise from the intervention. This list is not definitive, and the points made will not apply to all school-based projects which aim to support parents. The points are, rather, a guide to the lessons that have been learnt in the project, and the factors that should be borne in mind when undertaking similar projects in the future. The points made below relate to three areas, as follows:

- setting up, designing and running parent support projects in schools

- working effectively with parents and young people

- researching parent support projects.

Setting up, designing and running parent support projects in schools

The key learning points for future work are as follows:

- *It is essential to canvass the views of parents* before projects such as these are established, in order to ensure that the services offered meet parents' needs and preferences. Further, it is important to amend and develop the services offered during the course of the project, such as the decision made for the Parent Adviser to telephone all parents.

- *The school and the school's staff must be centrally involved* in the project: in this sort of parent support project, it is important to engage all the staff in it, enabling them to have a sense of ownership. The authors believe that while some school staff were centrally involved in the project, other staff should have been more actively involved.

- Linked to the point above, *school staff must be seen as the experts* about the parents and their relationship with the school. Thus, for example, the decision enabling the parent adviser to contact all parents individually was crucial to the success of this service, but was initially resisted from those outside the school setting.

- An important issue to consider in projects is *the age of the young people involved.* This project was limited to parents of 12–13-year-olds. It is of note that some parents felt that the project was offered too early for them, and that they would have preferred the project to be offered in two to three years' time, when their children were older. For others, however, it was clear that the timing of the project was just right. Further thought needs to be given to this issue. Clearly, offering such a project on a whole-school basis would meet the needs of parents with children of all ages.

- *Good communication must be maintained* by all those involved in this sort of project. For example, in the project described here those running the courses also encouraged parents to consult the parent adviser if they had a particular need, and the parent adviser ensured that parents had access to the materials when they wanted information on a particular topic. Linking different parts of the project in this way is important.

- *The project must be seen as relevant and useful to all parents.* It was clear that some parents at the school, as well as some members of staff, saw the project as being primarily for those with problems and difficulties. It should be stressed in projects such as this that all parents are likely to find something of use and interest in the services, and that all parents need information and support.

- *Consideration must be given to the location of the services offered.* In this project the group-based courses and the parent adviser were located in the school. Many parents thought this was a positive thing, in that both were easily accessible and on familiar ground. However, others clearly had concerns about confidentiality, and the visibility of attending a course or seeing the adviser. The possibility of locating these services outside of the school should be considered in future projects.

Working effectively with parents and young people

- *The importance of getting young people's views:* the young people in this intervention also completed questionnaires, giving their views about parenting and relationships. This was considered important, in particular as it provided a forum for explaining the project to the young people, and encouraging them to think about some of the issues their parents were exploring.

- There are clearly *other ways of engaging the young people in the project more directly,* such as offering courses for young people, or bringing parents and young people together in sessions. This could be done through drama work or the production of a newsletter.

- *Ways of including parents and young people equally* in the research process need to be explored. If the suggestions above are followed through, then it is also important to include young people to a greater extent in the evaluation. This might be done, for example, by interviewing some young people as well as parents, so that comparative data is available.

Researching parent support projects

A number of points about researching and evaluating parent support projects have already been made, and need to be reiterated here.

- *It is important to have contact with as many parents as possible at the beginning of the project,* preferably through individual interviews, and also to involve the young people as much as possible in the evaluation process.

- The project raised a number of issues about *what should be measured in parent support projects, and how this information should be collected.* In this sort of project it is not possible to identify a single outcome measure that can be used as the sole criterion for judging the success of the project. For example, for some parents, having information and feeling knowledgeable about adolescent development was a key outcome. For other parents what may be important is the opportunity to share and discuss with others. In the project described here, a broad range of measures were included, relating to knowledge, family relationships, feelings of support, use of services, and views of the services. All of these aspects are important in an evaluation of this sort.

- *It is particularly important to collect data from parents and young people both before and after the project.* Although this has implications for resources, it is preferable to undertaking the evaluation only after the project has been completed, as is often the case.

- *Some data needs to be collected from parents during the course of the project.* It was clear that some parents, by Time 2, could not remember events that took place during the course of the project. Thus, for example, some parents could not remember whether or not they had ordered any of the materials, and if so, what. Future interventions therefore need to undertake stages of the evaluation periodically throughout the project.

The following section offers some general conclusions about projects such as that described in the Fieldings School.

Conclusions

To end this chapter, it is useful to offer some general conclusions about the 'Living with Teenagers... Supporting Parents' project. It is considered that the project was successful in meeting its aims, in terms of providing information, help and support to a group of parents who are often isolated and unsupported. The impact of the project needs to be seen more broadly than this, however. The intervention has also enabled us to reflect on the broader processes involved in offering support to the parents of teenagers, particularly within specific contexts such as schools. The long list of points above is testimony to the learning that can result from this sort of innovative intervention.

In the introduction to the chapter it was said that the project emerged from a belief on the part of TSA (as well as others) that many parents of teenagers are isolated and unsupported, and that there is little consensus about the most effective ways of offering support to this group. The project has provided useful information in this respect, in particular in relation to the school context. The long-term effectiveness of the project in terms of preventing later problems and difficulties for families is not known.

However, it is reasonable to conjecture that the more information, advice and support parents receive, the less likely it is that difficulties will emerge later on. This is a key issue for future work.

One of the key aspects of the project, and one with real implications for future work, was the decision to offer three very different types of support services to the parents. This enabled parents to choose to use the service/s that they felt most comfortable with, and that would be most useful to them. This made the project truly innovative, and in keeping with current thinking about acknowledging difference and diversity among parents. This project was, however, very much a first step, and future work is needed to take these ideas forward.

TSA is currently working on a second project, designed to extend and develop some of the learning from the intervention described in this chapter. Characteristics of this project include:

- a school in a predominantly rural area

- parents of two year groups are involved – parents of 12–13-year-olds and 14–15-year-olds

- a much larger number of parents are participating (approximately 380 families in total)

- young people are involved in producing material for distribution to parents

- specific events are being organised for fathers

- greater flexibility has been built into the parent adviser role, including home visits.

This second project, which will be completed during 2001, will therefore provide new and valuable information about strategies to support parents of teenagers, using school-based interventions.

In concluding this chapter, the authors firmly believe that schools can be a very valuable setting for offering information and support to the parents of teenagers. Using school-based settings has the advantage of offering services to all parents in a particular year group, or indeed – resources permitting – in a school as a whole. Further work is needed to investigate the role of schools in offering support to the parents of teenagers.

References

Coleman, J. (1997) 'The parenting of teenagers in Britain today.' *Children and Society 11,* 45–52.

Roker, D. and Coleman, J. (1998) '"Parenting teenagers" programmes: A UK perspective.' *Children and Society 12,* 359–372.

Chapter 10

Professional Development in the Parenting Context

Mary Crowley

[The Parenting Education and Support Forum is referred to as PESF throughout this chapter for the sake of brevity.]

Introduction

There has been an explosion in work with parents since 1998 and a corresponding need for staff to deliver it. The demand for managers for new government initiatives such as Sure Start and On Track has created a career path with an increasing number of options for those who enjoy working with parents.

Funders have started to ask about quality assurance measures. Practitioners have become nervous about the possibility of 'cowboys' with no training or qualifications and little ability taking advantage of the increase in demand and proclaiming themselves expert in this area of work. The PESF's Training and Accreditation Working Group has been addressing these questions for some time, and has published training and accreditation guidelines (PESF 1999) which set out guidance on recruitment and a core curriculum for training parenting group facilitators. Much of the material in this chapter is based on the guidelines.

Practising what we preach

Providers of parenting education often encourage parents to model the behaviour they seek to encourage in their children. We tell parents attending parenting education groups how important it is to develop their support network and look after themselves, as well as developing and practising new skills and attitudes. Do we take our own messages to heart? Do we model the behaviour we are seeking to encourage in parents, and remember to seek support for ourselves and to develop and improve our own skills and attitudes? This chapter provides a few suggestions about how to do so.

Parents of teenagers

Parenting education is not like teaching woodwork or computer skills. Parents are vulnerable and deserve parent educators whose training and skills ensure that at the very least they will do no harm. The parents of teenagers often seem more desperate and, if anything, more fragile than other parents. They can feel more alone since they do not have the normal school-gate opportunities of younger children's parents to exchange worries and experiences. When they finally find a source of help from a parenting education and support provider, their needs may place a heavy burden on the provider.

The requirements for working safely with parents

Professor Hilton Davis (1999) sets out clearly four indispensable steps for ensuring safe and effective work with parents. People who work with parents, whether in a paid or voluntary capacity, need to:

- be carefully recruited
- receive appropriate and comprehensive initial training
- have access to a range of in-service development opportunities
- receive regular support and supervision.

In this chapter we shall look at the recruitment, training and supervision needs of providers of parenting education and support for the parents of teenagers, and give some examples of what is currently available. The final section will describe the work which the PESF is undertaking to identify national occupational standards because this will build the framework for professional development in this area in the future.

Recruitment

People can be trained in the skills needed to work with parents, but they must start with appropriate attitudes to the work. The PESF training and accreditation guidelines suggest that facilitators and other parent support workers should demonstrate:

- respect for members of the group
- respect for family and cultural diversity
- openness to a range of possible solutions to problems
- self-awareness and awareness of issues arising from our parenting experience
- demonstration of warm, empathetic personality
- maturity, self-confidence and the ability to listen to others.

These characteristics were also identified as crucial by providers who were interviewed for PESF by the Open University in 1999 as part of a survey (PESF/OU 2000) on the underlying skills, knowledge and attitudes needed in parenting educators:

> In the work that I do we often start with the experience of the parent, so one of the very important skills is being able to empathize, get into their shoes and give them permission to express what it's actually like, not to be too constrained by having to talk in a certain way. Finding a way of getting people to be real about what their problems are, what is really going on, and as part of that to convey that you are valuing them for themselves, not just because, not to subsume their identity within their relationship to the child, that they are an individual in their own right.

> The truth doesn't matter. It's the parents' perception of the truth that matters. It's what's going on for them and that's the place you've got to start...working alongside them, where they are, at that point in time. Then getting the course to jigsaw into that rather than doing it as a set piece event. I think that's the real skill...total empathy. Because that's about their reality. It's all about interpersonal skills and credibility. Because if you are a parent going to any course, if you don't gel with whoever is running the course for any reason, what you're going to pick up from it is going to be limited.

Evaluators of parenting education programmes often make the same point, that it's not the course which is selected that makes the difference, it's the quality of the person delivering it and the level of trust the parents feel in her (or, more rarely, him). What seems to be crucial is respect for the parents and a commitment to working alongside them. Not only is it the only approach which is acceptable to the vast majority of practitioners, it is underpinned by research, most recently that undertaken by Deborah Ghate (2001) for the Department of Health. The research she carried out with 1750 parents throughout Britain showed that control is the primary issue on parents' minds when seeking support. They want to be the ones who decide when, where, how and from whom they receive support. The parent must remain in charge. People who tend to know what is best for others should probably avoid working in the field of parenting education and support!

Where are parenting education and support workers recruited from?

The expansion in demand means that there are not enough suitable people already trained for work with parents. It is best to select for the right attitudes and qualities and train suitable recruits for the work. It can be tempting for hard-pressed managers and organisers to assume that someone trained to work with children automatically has the necessary personal qualities and skills to work with parents; or that expertise in a particular subject area, such as child health, confers the ability to work with parents. This may, of course, prove to be the case, but it is dangerous to take it for granted. Someone trained in a related area may already have covered some aspects of training for work with parents, but they may have development needs in other areas.

Recruitment for working with parents tends to be from two different sources, with different implications for training and professional development. The first source is those parents who themselves have benefited from parenting education and feel they would like to go on to help others in the same way. This can be a very powerful model. Parents often say that they prefer to receive help and support from people who are themselves parents. Where the parents have experienced difficulties very similar to those faced by those they are helping, it tends to encourage them to approach others' problems in a respectful and exploratory way, conscious that there are no easy solutions. They excel in the 'crucial core skill of empathy' identified by the Open University survey respondent quoted above. These parent providers will probably need initial training in all of the core areas identified by the PESF guidelines and described below, unless they happen to have had this training already for a related area of work.

The second group of workers in the parenting field are those professionals trained for a related area who propose to develop their work with parents, and need training specifically for that purpose. These include, for example, school nurses, probation officers and schoolteachers. There are others whose normal work is with parents but who may want to develop a particular aspect, such as group work, for which they need additional training. These include health visitors, education welfare officers and social workers.

Training

There is a minimum of initial training which needs to be undertaken by anyone embarking on running parenting groups for 'ordinary' parents. (Longer training will be required for working in specialist settings or with groups with a higher level of need.) The core training areas set out in the PESF guidelines are as follows:

- recruiting parents and administering the course
- facilitating parenting skills
- working collaboratively
- providing opportunities for participants to reflect on their own experiences as children, partners and parents
- giving out information
- identifying sources of further support for parents where appropriate
- building a local personal referral network
- making arrangements for supervision and support for facilitator/group leader.

Additional recommended training

As well as acquiring these core skills and knowledge, PESF recommends that facilitators should have an opportunity to reflect on how their own experiences of being parented, and of being parents, may affect their interaction with parents. They also need a chance to practise modelling the interpersonal skills and attitudes which they wish to help parents develop, for example, listening, negotiating, respect, and valuing existing skills, knowledge and experience. They should make clear the belief system and values which underpin their approach to parenting. Last, we think it is crucial that they obtain support and supervision for themselves and become familiar with services to which parents can be referred if necessary.

Identifying training needs

Training for anyone undertaking the delivery of education and support to parents should cover at least the minimum core areas set out above. Some aspects are already covered by the professional training of some groups; for example, trained adult educators will be familiar with the group enabling skills, and child development forms part of the training of health visitors and others. Parent educator training should therefore acknowledge and, where appropriate, offer accreditation for prior learning so that trainees need not cover aspects twice. As trainees come from a variety of backgrounds and deliver courses in a variety of settings, each training course should be designed for the target group of trainees.

Additional training needs for those working with parents of teenagers

Practitioners working specifically with parents of teenagers often feel more confident if they have had training in the following areas:

- adolescent development

- recruiting and working with fathers

- information about sex and relationships education, teenage pregnancy, contraception, abortion and sexually transmitted diseases

- helping parents deal with examination pressure or worries about their young person's schooling

- eating disorders

- drugs: information about the law, how to recognise common types of drugs, availability, dangers and cost, recommendations of drugs education experts

- awareness of the difference in approach to growing up and leaving home in different cultural communities

- knowledge of youth crime legislation.

Training for different career pathways

It is interesting to look at the kind of jobs and career structures that now exist in parenting education and support.

If we take as a base-line the job of facilitating a group of 'good enough' parents, with no specific pre-identified problems, it is possible to identify at least three career progression routes which could be taken. These are: managing the project that is providing those 'good enough parent' groups; facilitating groups with specific problems (for example, parents of young offenders, or parents who are themselves drug abusers); or taking the academic route and becoming a researcher or provider of training for others. Different training would be required to enable someone to do each of these three jobs. A trainee's choice will also take into consideration issues like the cost of training, length of training, and whether supervision arrangements are in place. The trainee also needs to decide if accreditation is important.

Training needs of Youth Offending Teams

When Youth Offending Teams (YOTs) were given the task of implementing Parenting Orders in June 2000, there was considerable anxiety expressed by some about what they perceived as their lack of skills and experience for the work. At a seminar convened in April 2000 by PESF and the Trust for the Study of Adolescence (TSA) for those YOTs embarking on the work for the first time, it was noticeable that the underlying attitudes of treating parents with respect and seeking to work with them in an empowering way were very much part of the work ethos of those YOT members attending. They felt that what they needed was training in specific parenting skills, in assessing parents' needs, and in group-work techniques.

Where YOTs have subcontracted the delivery of the parenting education to local authority, health authority or voluntary sector providers, YOT members require training only in assessing parents' needs to enable them to offer individual or group-based help, some form of family therapy, or another appropriate intervention. Practitioners say that the assessment can be a very delicate process: parents can feel desperate and at the end of their tether and they are quick to resent any approach which they see as blaming them or offering unrealistic solutions.

In-service training

Because of the varied pattern of recruitment to parenting education and support, what would be initial training for some providers will be in-service training for others who embark on work with parents long after they have completed training for some other area. As well as undertaking the core areas of training identified above, it would be useful for all providers to have access to in-service training opportunities covering topics like:

- main findings from new research
- working with specific target groups, for example, parents of children with disabilities, or gay and lesbian parents
- keeping up to date with new initiatives
- dealing with specific aspects such as step-families
- improving cultural awareness
- working with the parents of teenage parents
- working with teenage parents.

Some specialised aspects of work with parents should be undertaken only where practitioners have had specific additional training – for example, where parents have learning difficulties, or where there are child protection issues.

We strongly urge that whenever possible there should be joint training sessions at local level for all those working with families. In addition to learning about the subject-matter of the training, the participants get to know each other, become familiar with each other's work, identify possible savings and other benefits through working together, and are enabled to ensure more coherent provision for parents.

Accreditation

Accredited or non-accredited training?

It is possible for training to be first-class without being formally accredited. As the field of work grows, employers and managers who wish to provide education and support for parents are, however, seeking the assurance of quality afforded by employing staff who have undertaken recognised, accredited training. There is also an increasing demand from those undertaking training that it should lead to transferable accreditation. Accreditation needs to be transferable, that is to have national validity, so that it will be recognised outside the geographical area or provider organisation. It needs to be able to form part of the trainee's training portfolio.

Accreditation and funding

Accredited courses became popular with provider organisations a few years ago when the principal funder of post–16 education and training, the Further Education Funding Council, offered funding for training, conditional on the training's offering nationally recognised qualifications. From April 2001 the national funding structure changed again when all post–16 education and training (apart from higher education at universities) became the responsibility of the national and local Learning and Skills Councils. These bodies are empowered to fund both accredited and non-accredited training. It seems unlikely, however, that they will wish to depart from the path followed by their predecessors in encouraging accredited training.

Link to national childcare qualifications framework

There is now an opportunity to develop a national accreditation model for parenting education and support, linked to the national qualifications framework for work in early years and childcare which has been developed by the Qualifications and Curriculum Authority in England and sister organisations in Scotland, Wales and Northen Ireland. This opportunity will be seized by PESF and its partner national training organisation, PAULO (the national training organisation for community-based learning and development), because many practitioners cross between the two areas of work and would find compatible accreditation systems invaluable.

Accreditation of training for working with parents can be at pre-university level or at university level. There is a demand for both options. University-accredited training is popular with providers who are already graduates or the equivalent, or who are working towards a degree. These include all nurses, health visitors, social workers, teachers, many adult and community education lecturers and members of YOTs.

Examples of university-accredited training

Examples of university accredited provision are:

EXETER

From October 2001 the University of Exeter will offer a degree in working with parents with learning difficulties.

DE MONTFORT UNIVERSITY/PESF

The De Montfort/PESF accreditation was developed to provide a means for workers, often volunteers already linked with parenting organisations, to gain university-level recognition of their training and experience.

Four modules, devised by a working group from PESF and De Montfort University (DMU), have been validated by the university. The modules are:

1. Planning and facilitating parenting groups

2. Empowering parents: facilitating parenting skills

3. Lifespan I: Infancy to childhood: the developing child and the developing parent

4. Lifespan II: Adolescence to adulthood: the developing young person and the developing parent

All are undergraduate Level One modules. In order to achieve university validation, the requirements for the first two modules and at least one of the others need to be met. These modules are designed for work with parents of 'ordinary' children. DMU is also developing with PESF a range of qualifications for parents of 'troubled' teenagers.

Parenting organisations who are already training people to work as facilitators for groups of parents are able to map their curricula for training facilitators against the validated curricula, and if there is broad correspondence, they are able to receive a 'letter of recognition' from DMU. Organisations are then in a position to encourage their facilitators, once they have undertaken their own organisation's course of education and training, to apply to become external students of DMU and to complete the assessment requirements for one or more modules.

PIPPIN (PARENTS IN PARTNERSHIP – PARENT–INFANT NETWORK)

Pippin offers university-level accreditation of its modular Dip HE/Bsc (Hons) in Facilitation of Parent–Infant Relationships, accredited by the

University of Hertfordshire. This may be of interest to those currently working with parents of teenagers but thinking of transferring to parents of a much younger age group or expectant parents.

Non-university-level training

Community-based providers often include parents who are not ready to undertake university-level courses of study. They may have had a low initial level of educational attainment, or may not have been able to afford the cost or the time involved. If they want to undertake training which leads to accreditation, their requirements are better met by accreditation at NVQ Level 3 or the equivalent, which approximates to A-level. Lower equivalent levels would be unlikely to be appropriate since NVQ Level 3 is called for in any work where the practitioner works without supervision. This is clearly the case in parenting education and support, whether the practitioner is working with parents individually or in groups.

Supervision and Support

Management or supportive supervision?

I am using the term 'supervision' here to mean an opportunity for a practitioner to reflect with a manager, colleague or fellow practitioner on her/his practice in working with parents; to explore difficulties and solutions; to express the positive and negative emotions which the work gives rise to; to discharge the burden of supporting parents in order to improve the capacity to work effectively. To avoid confusion, I shall refer to this type of supervision as 'supportive supervision' in the rest of this chapter.

Clearly, for providers who are working for an organisation, there is also a need for management supervision, in the sense of a manager considering the work of a staff member so as to determine whether it is delivering the intended outcomes, resolve practical matters and plan future work. It is rarely appropriate for supportive supervision to be carried out by the line manager. Someone who is sufficiently outside the work to be capable of detachment best provides this.

A range of supportive supervision

The purpose of supervision is to improve practitioners' capacity to work more effectively. A range of supportive supervision could include the following:

- professional supervision from someone with counselling or psychotherapy training
- formal peer supervision from a fellow practitioner
- opportunities for informal, face-to-face or telephone conversations with a colleague or fellow practitioner
- group supervision.

Peer supervision may be useful in many cases. It can, however, be difficult for peers to challenge each other, should that seem to be necessary. The supervisor needs the capacity to listen carefully and understand what are the real, sometimes hidden, concerns of the person having supervision.

It could be very valuable to have occasional opportunities to talk to someone with professional training in child and adolescent development and psychotherapy or counselling, and to have their view about what is really going on for the parents. The parenting provider is dealing with powerful feelings which may trigger uncomfortable or distressing responses in him/herself. If s/he feels anxious or distressed, s/he may tend to dismiss or minimise what a parent is saying. The supervisor needs to be able to help parenting providers to identify their own needs arising from their own experience.

Good supervision can help the provider think at the deeper or macro-level. It provides additional links into what is going on in the field. The supervisor can suggest additional reading and help the practitioner to learn and develop. It is an indispensable part of in-service training. Providers themselves will decide what form and frequency of supervision and support would be most useful to them.

Paying for supportive supervision

Supervision need not cost a huge amount. The cost could be met in a number of ways, for example: an existing salaried staff member can include it as part of their duties; reciprocal peer supervision can be arranged at low cost; group supervision sessions can enable a number of practitioners to receive supervision at the same time and to learn from each other's experience. Practitioners new to delivering education and support for parents are likely to need supervision more frequently than more experienced providers. Supervision is not directly linked to volume of work, since a provider offering a large number of sessions with parents may need the same supervision as someone delivering only one session a week. What is crucial is that supervision is seen as an indispensable part of working with parents and is written into initial planning.

National quality standards

PESF is committed to ensuring that the training and accreditation structures developed for parenting education and support staff are part of the mainstream of national developments. This is particularly important since work with parents attracts people from related areas such as childcare, health, psychotherapy or education, who want portable qualifications with national currency which will enable them to have flexible career patterns.

National training organisations

National occupational standards for a particular area of work set out the minimum expectations for how that work is carried out. The Department for Education and Employment (Dfee), in partnership with employers, has put in place a structure of national training organisations (NTOs) which have responsibility for the development, review and implementation of national occupational standards for specified sectors and occupations. NTOs exist, for example, for the food and drink industry, the voluntary sector, social work, banking and building societies, arts and entertainment. They number 64 at time of writing.

PAULO: lead for parenting education and support

The lead NTO for work with parents is PAULO, the NTO for community-based learning and development. PESF is working in close partnership with PAULO to identify national standards for work with parents. This work is urgently needed because there is considerable anxiety among experienced parenting educators that the welcome increase in the volume of work with parents, and the consequent demand for more workers, may result in a lowering of standards. The existing pool of skilled and experienced people is being recruited to fill posts in YOTs, Sure Start, On Track and Early Years Partnership. The small amount of training available at present for this area cannot deliver enough suitable people to keep pace with demand. The task of identifying the national standards will be carried out in partnership with those who work in the sector and will involve colleagues in Scotland, Wales and Northern Ireland as well as England, because national standards must be applicable to all four countries.

It is necessary for us to be clear about whether standards which have already been identified can meet the needs of our occupational sector. To judge that, PESF, in partnership with PAULO, has commissioned work to draw an occupational map identifying in what context parenting education and support takes place and what employment areas need to be involved, to consult employers and practitioners about the map, to carry out a functional analysis of education and support for parents, and to identify any existing standards which apply to the work. Should we identify any gaps in existing standards, it will then be necessary to draft new standards to fill them and consult the sector about the new standards.

Implications of the standards for the provision of training

The standards are precisely what their name suggests: pre-determined levels of expertise and good practice for the delivery of the work. They are urgently needed to ensure that the increasing work with parents is of a high quality and is accompanied by a corresponding increase in opportunities for training and staff development. It is certain that much existing work is excellent and will meet the national standards when they have been identified. Some providers, however, will want to undertake further training to enable them to reach the standard. There is a problem in the short supply of training providers. PESF is urging the Learning and Skills Councils nationally and locally to commit funding to providing a variety of training opportunities for the delivery of parenting education and support.

Looking forward

Recognition by policy-makers that parenting can be improved by education and support is a significant step forward. It is now easier to imagine a future where parents receive the help and support they need before they have children and at each stage of a child's development. PESF is anxious that the growth in provision for the parents of teenagers be accompanied by employers' insistence on careful recruitment and initial training, an increase in opportunities for in-service training, and routine provision of supportive supervision. The fact that people come to working with parents by a variety of routes makes the availability of professional development opportunities particularly important in enabling practitioners to identify and address their specific skills and experience gaps.

Work with parents is enriched by the varied backgrounds of different practitioners from the health sector, community safety, youth justice, education, or parents who have themselves attended community-based, voluntary sector provision. There is now an exciting opportunity to agree common principles to secure the quality of all work with parents and to ensure that the national standards enshrine the ethos of treating parents with respect.

References

Davis, H. (1999) Lecture, Queen Mary and Westfield College, 15 June 1999.

The Parenting Education and Support Forum (1999) *Parenting Education and Support: Guidelines on Training and Accreditation.* London: National Children's Bureau Enterprises Ltd.

Ghate, D. (2001) *Parenting in Poor Environments*, a study by the Policy Research Bureau for the Department of Health.

PESF/Open University (2000): Report on project to assess the training needs of people working with parents and primary carers, by Jan Atkins in consultation with Martin Robb. Unpublished.

Chapter 11

The Parenting of Teenagers
Present and Future
Debi Roker and John Coleman

In this final chapter we review some of the key issues raised by the contributors to this book. We will also make some general comments about the parenting of teenagers and strategies to offer support to this group of parents. We will do this by addressing two key questions: first, what have we learnt from these chapters, and what do they tell us about current work to support the parents of teenagers? Second, where do we go from here? How can policy and practice in this area best move forward? We will start by identifying the main learning points from these chapters.

What have we learnt from these chapters?

The contributors to this book have addressed a wide range of issues, each from different perspectives, professional standpoints and experience. The content of the chapters has also been diverse and has included information about research, good practice, work with parents in specific contexts (and with specific groups of parents), and the results of interventions. Each has provided valuable information which is likely to be of considerable value to professionals working with families. A number of important learning points can be derived from the chapters. These are:

THE PARENTING OF TEENAGERS MATTERS

All the chapters have highlighted the fact that the parenting of teenagers is important, with significant implications for young people's health and wellbeing, as well as for the functioning of families. As we demonstrated in

Chapter 1, support for parents in the UK has historically focused on the parents of young children, with little attention given to the needs and experience of the parents of teenagers (Coleman 1997). All the chapters have demonstrated that, while provision is still patchy, there is now a much more concerted effort to focus on the needs of this group of parents. This new focus is important, and needs to be extended and developed. (See below, 'Where do we go from here?'.)

WORK TO SUPPORT PARENTS OF TEENAGERS IS INCREASING

Related to the previous point, the chapters in this book have demonstrated the increasing amount of work that is now taking place to support the parents of teenagers. This work is taking place in a variety of different sectors, including education (see, for example, Chapter 9), the health service (Chapter 7), the youth justice system (Chapters 4 and 5), and the community and voluntary sectors (Chapters 3 and 8). These developments are of course very welcome, and it is undoubtedly true that much of this has been encouraged and initiated by the present Labour government. We consider it an important task for the future to both develop and evaluate these initiatives. Extending this work into other settings, such as general practice or the workplace, is also likely to prove fruitful.

PARENTS HAVE DIFFERENT NEEDS

One of the key conclusions is that parents of teenagers are very diverse, and service provision must reflect this diversity. As we demonstrated in the first two chapters, parents' needs and experiences differ according to their family structure, income, housing, class, ethnicity, employment status, gender and a large number of other factors. These different circumstances and needs must be reflected in service provision. Thus, for example, Chapter 3 describes the circumstances of black and minority ethnic families in Britain in the twenty-first century, and emphasises the need to be responsive to culture and ethnicity in providing services for parents of teenagers. Chapter 9 describes a project aimed at a deprived, working-class community and highlights the differences between this and another project taking place in a middle-class rural school. Further work is needed to explore the needs of different groups of parents, and how different family, personal and cultural circumstances impact on parenting.

DIVERSITY OF PROVISION

Reflecting the diversity of parenting needs and experiences identified above, the chapters have demonstrated the importance of offering a diversity of provision. In the past, support for parents was sometimes viewed very narrowly as the provision of, for example, a group-based course, or materials to take home. These chapters have demonstrated much broader thinking about provision for this group of parents. Chapter 8, for example, showed the importance of looking at different ways of drawing parents in to parenting support projects, and offering a wide range of different types of activities. Similarly, Chapters 5, 6 and 9 demonstrated the importance of diversity of provision. In particular, these chapters show that while some parents want to be involved with other parents (for example via group-based courses or events), others want sources of support that they can use in their own homes (such as videos and materials), or on a one-to-one basis (such as a parent adviser, or via a telephone helpline). In thinking about diversity of provision, these different formats of support must be considered.

NEGATIVE IMAGES OF PARENTING SUPPORT

Several contributors have made the point that seeking help and advice about parenting is sometimes seen as a sign of failure (Chapters 7 and 8). While the situation has undoubtedly improved over the last few years, there is still a pervasive image of parenting support being primarily for those parents who are in difficulty. This situation has not been helped by the introduction of Parenting Orders, which links one of the main forms of parenting support (group-based courses) to involvement in the youth justice system. Several of the chapters have also, however, identified ways of making support for parents more universally accepted, and as being of relevance to all parents. This issue is discussed further in the following section.

PURPOSES OF PARENT SUPPORT

The chapters in this book have made a significant contribution to a key question in this field, about the *purpose* of providing support for parents. In a useful contribution, Jones (1999) distinguishes between three discourses in relation to parenting support: empowerment, promotion and prevention. The book has explored parenting support within each of these discourses. Uitterdijk and Pitt, for example, report parenting support projects which aim primarily to empower parents, but which also aim to promote better parenting (Chapter 8); Davis and Day report on the parent adviser model, which aims to promote more effective parenting and also to prevent later problems (Chapter 7). Chapter 5 by Lindfield and Cusick, describing work with parents in the youth justice context, falls primarily within the preventive discourse.

Attempts to categorise the various purposes of parenting support are important, as they help us to focus on why a particular type of support is planned, and who it might be most appropriate for. However, it is also important to acknowledge that most parenting support projects have a number of different aims, many of which will fall into all three of the categories described above. Chapter 9, by Roker and Richardson, for example, describes a project where all three of these discourses were used to describe the aim of the intervention. (See also Roker, Richardson and Coleman (2000) for further discussion of this point.)

FOCUSING ON THE POSITIVE

A number of contributors have commented on the fact that there are largely negative stereotypes of young people and the teenage years. There is thus an expectation that teenagers will be difficult, and that the teenage years will probably be taxing and unfulfilling for parents. However, research evidence points to a very different conclusion. As Coleman demonstrates in Chapter 2, research shows that, despite the changes the adolescent years bring, most parents report positive experiences of this time, despite any difficulties encountered. Further, there is often little acknowledgement in discussions about teenagers of the positive changes that the adolescent years bring, including such aspects as greater independence among young people, more self-awareness and self-determination. It is important that future work to support the parents of teenagers does not focus exclusively on negative, difficult experiences, but rather presents a balanced view of the changes that occur at this time. This will, in turn, contribute towards the normalisation of accessing help and advice at this time.

DIFFERENT STRATEGIES FOR ENGAGING PARENTS

Several chapters have identified ways of encouraging parents of teenagers to access advice and support services, and see it as a normal, positive aspect of parenting. In Chapter 8, for example, Uitterdijk and Pitt describe a number of ways in which one-off sessions and courses can be made attractive to parents, using strategies such as focusing on the parents' own experiences of growing up, and by making events welcoming and non-threatening. These authors also discuss the nature of 'hooks' into parenting support, such as sport, fun and nostalgia, and the learning of new skills. Similarly, Box, in Chapter 3, focuses on black and minority ethnic families, and ways of ensuring that services are applicable and relevant to this group of parents. She outlines a number of strategies being used by the Race Equality Unit in projects to engage black and minority ethnic families in parent support work. In Chapter 6 Braun focuses on the use of helplines as a source of support, and also indicates how important anonymity is to some parents. Her chapter is an important reminder that not all parent support work has to be face-to-face; there are many parents who prefer to access support in an anonymous way.

MATERIALS AVAILABLE TO SUPPORT PARENTS

It is of note that only a few years ago there were very few resources available for the parents of teenagers. As a result, there were few resources for professionals working with this group of parents. There are now significantly more resources available, including materials for group-based courses, books, videos and newsletters. However, many of these are not well known, and word-of-mouth is often the most common form of dissemination. It is in many ways ironic that, as Lindfield and Cusick demonstrate in Chapter 5, some of the most significant developments in terms of materials have been within the youth justice field. It is important that information about resources is distributed more widely. A useful start to this has been made by the Parenting Education and Support Forum (PESF). Further, materials and information needs to be provided in new forms. At the Trust for the Study of Adolescence (TSA), we are investigating the use of newsletters as a form of support for parents. Websites also offer considerable possibilities, and could be a good source of information and support. There is likely to be a growth in these forms of support in the future.

Where do we go from here?

The points detailed above describe the current situation in relation to supporting the parents of teenagers. In this final section, we aim to offer some ideas and suggestions in relation to future policy and practice in this area.

NORMALISING PARENT SUPPORT

As mentioned above, it is important that all those involved in this area of work are able to promote the 'normalisation' of parenting support. While considerable strides have been made in recent years, a more concerted campaign is needed – particularly in the media – to promote the idea that all parents can benefit from information and support. It is essential that accessing support is not equated with 'failure', but is seen instead as a positive and natural activity.

INCREASING THE FOCUS ON THE NEEDS OF PARENTS OF TEENAGERS

While the contributions to this book provide testimony to the increased attention being given to the parents of teenagers, there is a long way to go before a proper balance is achieved. Parents of babies and young children still receive far greater resources and attention than the parents of teenagers. This imbalance is perhaps inevitable, given the importance of the early years for establishing patterns of behaviour relationships. However, the changes and developments that occur in the adolescent years (as detailed in Chapter 2) demonstrate the need to provide more support for this group of parents. It is essential that the current range of provision for parents of teenagers is developed and extended. It should be noted here that the funding provided by the Home Office Family Policy Unit over recent years has been particularly valuable in this respect, encouraging a renewed focus on practical ways of supporting parents of teenagers.

INCREASING THE VARIETY OF SUPPORT AVAILABLE

The contributors have highlighted a number of novel and valuable approaches for providing the parents of teenagers with information and support. All the chapters have demonstrated how important it is to offer a variety of strategies, so that parents can use the kind that they feel is most useful to them, and with which they feel most comfortable. This could be having access to printed materials or videos, telephone helplines, websites, group-based programmes, or one-off events. Each of these sources of support needs to be developed and extended, so that all parents can have access to them. This would clearly be expensive, and would require a financial commitment by the government to increased levels of support for this group of parents.

CLARIFY THE PARENT–TEENAGER RELATIONSHIP

Some of the recent developments in parent support work have brought into sharp focus the relationship between parents and young people. Jones and Bell (2000) have highlighted some of the contradictions inherent in current legislation involving young people (see also Chapter 2 in this volume). Thus, for example, while much political discourse focuses on the importance of young people becoming more mature and increasingly responsible for their own behaviour, this is in sharp contrast to recent legislative changes, many of which make parents legally responsible for the actions of their teenagers. This area is in urgent need of clarification and would, in turn, enable parents and young people to clarify their relationship.

BROADEN SUPPORT FOR PARENTS OF OLDER TEENAGERS

As demonstrated by Coleman in Chapter 2, the adolescent period is now longer than it used to be. In particular, many young people are now staying at home long into their twenties, and even beyond. This change needs to be borne in mind when providing support for parents. How does the parenting of a 15-year-old, for example, differ from having a 22-year-old in the home? Indeed, very little is known about the relationship between parents and older children living at home. Support systems need to be developed that take these changes in family life into consideration.

GREATER RECOGNITION OF GENDER IN PARENTING SUPPORT WORK

There is clear evidence that most projects to support parents of teenagers are overwhelmingly used by mothers. It is important that the issue of fathers and fathering is addressed in future work to support parents. Specific projects for fathers need to be offered (such as those currently being run by the YMCA), to encourage fathers to participate more fully. It is likely that quite different strategies will be needed to engage fathers in parenting support projects.

FINDING OUT WHAT WORKS

It is clear from the contributions to this book that there are now many different approaches and strategies being offered to support the parents of teenagers. What is also clear, however, is that very little formal evaluation has been undertaken of many of these projects. This is a significant omission, as without formal evaluations, projects may be continuing

204 / SUPPORTING PARENTS OF TEENAGERS

without any information about their effectiveness or value to parents. Finding out 'what works' and for whom, is a crucial task for the future. We would propose that in all new projects aimed at the parents of teenagers, an evaluation element is included.

In making this proposal, we would also raise the issue of 'outcomes' in parenting support work. Thus, for example, a parent may report having enjoyed a group-based parenting course, and found it interesting to listen to the views of others. However, this does not mean that their communication skills, for example, have necessarily improved, or that attending the course led to changes in their relationship with their teenager, or indeed in the behaviour of their daughter or son. Establishing clear outcomes for evaluations of parent support work is essential. It is an issue that we have raised many times, particularly in relation to the evaluation of interventions (Roker and Coleman 1998; Roker, Richardson and Coleman 2000). In previous work we have highlighted the need for evaluations to distinguish between outcomes such as: parents' *enjoyment* of a project, the *knowledge* they gain from it (about themselves, their parenting, and about adolescent development), their level of *confidence* in their parenting, their feelings of *support*, and actual *changes* in their behaviour, their relationship with their children, and their teenager's behaviour. Evaluations of projects to support the parents of teenagers need to be refined and developed, in particular with regard to being clear about which of these elements is being measured. In addition, more longitudinal evaluations need to be undertaken in order to identify the long-term effectiveness of such interventions. Only with this evidence will policy-makers be persuaded to invest additional time and resources to support this group of parents.

THE 'PROFESSIONALISATION' OF PARENT SUPPORT

In Chapter 10, Mary Crowley explores issues of accreditation in relation to parent support work. This is an important issue, and one which is receiving increasing recognition, reflecting the greater 'professionalisation' of this field. There is a growing debate about who should be providing parenting support, and the amount (and type) of training that they should receive. Indeed, the authors have been witness to many a debate on this topic. Some in this field believe that, for example, to run a group-based course the only real qualification needed is to be the parent of a teenager, and the only facilities needed are some good materials and a comfortable venue. Others are completely opposed to this, believing that course facilitators should be qualified and experienced in group-work and other professional skills. The 'professionalisation' of parent support work is a crucial topic of debate for the future, and one where further work is needed.

INVOLVING YOUNG PEOPLE

An increasingly important issue in relation to the parenting of teenagers is the extent to which young people themselves are involved. Most strategies for supporting parents, whether courses, helplines, or materials, have been for parents alone, and have not involved young people. Increasingly, however, workers in this field are trying also to involve young people, viewing this as both empowering young people and engaging the 'other half' of the equation. Such projects are, however, relatively rare, and nothing is available on a national basis. Some examples of projects which involve parents and young people within the youth justice arena are discussed in Chapter 5 by Lindfield and Cusick and also in Roker, Richardson and Coleman (2000). Further work is needed in this important area, including the evaluation of such novel interventions.

Conclusion

In the first two chapters we highlighted the fact that, historically, much more attention and resources have been devoted to the parenting of babies and young children than to the parenting of teenagers. We also demonstrated, however, the different needs of the parents of teenagers, and the different issues that are faced by the parents of this age group. This concluding chapter has identified some of the main points and issues raised by the different contributors to this book. We have also highlighted some of the key issues that need to be addressed in future work in this area. The book was written primarily for practitioners, and aimed to combine information about research with up-to-date ideas and strategies from key figures working in this area. Further work needs to be undertaken to share information about research and practice between all those involved in this crucial field.

References

Coleman, J. (1997) 'The parenting of teenagers in Britain today.' *Children and Society 11*, 45–52.

Jones, G. and Bell, R. (2000) *Balancing Acts: Youth, Parenting and Public Policy*. York: Joseph Rowntree Foundation.

Jones, P. (1999) 'Parenting education and support: Issues in multi-agency collaboration.' In S. Wolfendale and H. Einzig (eds) *Parenting Education and Support.* London: David Fulton.

Roker, D. and Coleman, J. (1998) '"Parenting teenagers" programmes: A UK perspective.' *Children and Society* 12, 359–372.

Roker, D., Richardson, H. and Coleman, J. (2000) *Innovations in Parenting Support: An evaluation of the YMCA's 'Parenting Teenagers' Programme.* London: YMCA.

Useful Addresses

Adlerian Family and Teacher Education Centre (AFTEC)
43 Rectory Road
Oxford
OX4 1BU
Provides training in Adlerian approach for those running courses

Care for the Family
PO Box 488
Cardiff
CF15 7YY
0292 081 0800
Provides information and materials on parenting

Centre for Fun and Families
25 Shanklin Drive
Knighton
Leicester
LE2 3RH
0116 270 7198
www.comcom.org.uk
Provides materials and training for those running courses

Eileen Murphy Consultants
227a Martin Way
London
SW20 9BU
0208 542 9310
Training and consultancy

Family Caring Trust
8 Ashtree Enterprise Park
Newry
Co. Down
BT34 1BY
028 3026 4174
www.familycaring.co.uk
Produces materials for use on courses

Let's Talk Parenting

Pentaxion Ltd
180 Bridge Street
Newcastle-Upon-Tyne, NE1 2TE
0191 232 6189
Provides materials and training

Merton College

Parenting Development Department
Merton College
Morden Park
London Road
Morden
Surrey
SM4 5QX
0208 640 3001
www.merton.ac.uk
Provides training for those running courses, including specialist training for those working in the youth justice system

National Family and Parenting Institute (NFPI)

520 Highgate Studios
53–79 Highgate Road
Kentish Town
London
NW5 1TL
0207 424 3460
www.nfpi.org.uk
National organisation undertaking research and policy development in relation to families and parenting

Parenting Connections

14 Somali Road
London
NW2 3RL
0207 813 9190
Consultancy and training

Parenting Education and Support Forum (PESF)

Unit 431, Highgate Studios
53–79 Highgate Road
Kentish Town
NW5 1TL
0207 284 8380
www.parenting-forum.org.uk
Umbrella organisation for all those who work with parents, providing information, resources, training

Parentline Plus

Unit 520, Highgate Studios
53–79 Highgate Road
London
NW5 1TL
0207 209 2460
www.parentlineplus.org.uk
Provides information, runs Parentline telephone helpline, organises courses and workshops

Promoting Effective Parenting

5 Walsingham Place
Truro
Cornwall
TR21 2RP
01872 263334
Offers inter-agency training in assessment of children, young people and families

Race Equality Unit (REU)

Unit 27/28, Angel Gate
City Road
London
EC1V 2PT
0207 278 2331
www.reunet.demon.co.uk
Undertakes research and produces materials in relation to black and ethnic minority parents and parenting

Trust for the Study of Adolescence (TSA)

23 New Road
Brighton
East Sussex
BN1 1WZ
01273 693311
www.tsa.uk.com
Undertakes research and produces/sells materials in relation to parenting

Y-Touring

10 Lennox Road
London
N4 3NW
0207 272 5755
www.ytouring.org.uk
National theatre company of the YMCA, produces plays on parenting

YMCA 'Dads and Lads' project

YMCA England
Dee Bridge House
25–27 Lower Bridge Street
Chester
CH1 1RS
01244 403090
National project combining sport with parenting sessions

Contributors

Leandra Box is currently a Research Fellow at REU. Leandra was involved in adapting the Strengthening Families, Strengthening Communities Parent Programme for use with black and minority ethnic communities in the UK and is currently co-ordinating the Black and Minority Ethnic Family Policy Forum. Leandra has published widely on social care and family centres.

Dorit Braun has long experience of parenting education and training professionals in family support. She has worked in Adult and Community Education and as a Locality Commissioner in a Health Authority. She then went on to become Chief Executive of the National Stepfamily Association, successfully guiding the organisation through merger with Parent Network and Parentline UK, to form Parentline Plus. In June 2000 Dorit was awarded an OBE on the Queen's birthday honours list for her services to parenting. Dorit is a single parent to three sons.

John Coleman is founder and Director of the Trust for the Study of Adolescence, an independent applied research and training organisation based in Brighton. His background is as a clinical and educational psychologist. John has a long-standing interest in strategies to support parents of teenagers, and has produced a wide range of books, audio-tapes and videos for both parents and professionals.

Mary Crowley is Chief Executive of the Parenting Education & Support Forum, the national umbrella organisation for people who work with parents. Prior to joining the Forum, she was Head of the Adult Education Service in the east London Borough of Waltham Forest, and Director of the EU Socrates DIALOGUE parenting education programme with partners in six European countries. She has three sons, two daughters and one step-son.

Janice Cusick is a Co-ordinator for Parenting and Youth Justice at the Trust for the Study of Adolescence, and has been providing support to 42 parenting projects funded under the Youth Justice Board's Intervention Programme. Janice's background is in health: visiting, promotion and education. She has worked as a health secondee on a Youth Offending Team running parenting groups. Janice has a special interest in working with the challenging behaviour of young people, particularly in a family therapy context. Janice is about to undertake the Diploma in Applied Systemic Therapy, having completed the Certificate course at the Tavistock and Portman NHS Trust in London.

Hilton Davis is a consultant clinical psychologist with the South London and Maudsley NHS Trust, where he is the Director of the Centre for Parent and Child Support, a consultancy, training and research centre for the development of family services. He is also Professor of Child Health Psychology at the Guy's, King's and St Thomas' School of Medicine, King's College, University of London. He is particularly interested in finding and evaluating ways of facilitating the psychosocial support role for all professions working with children and parents.

Crispin Day is a consultant clinical psychologist working for the South London and Maudsley NHS Trust. He is Head of the Southwark Community Child and Family Service and a consultant in the Centre for Parent and Child Support. He specialises in the development, evaluation and dissemination of community child mental health services.

Clem Henricson is the Policy and Research Manager at the National Family and Parenting Institute. She was formerly Head of Crime and Social Policy at NACRO and an adviser to the Association of London Authorities. More recently she has been a consultant working with the Home Office, the Youth Justice Board, the Trust for the Study of Adolescence and the Family Policy Studies Centre. She has published widely on family policy.

Sarah Lindfield is a Co-ordinator for Parenting and Youth Justice at the Trust for the Study of Adolescence, and has been providing support to 42 parenting projects funded under the Youth Justice Board's Intervention Programme. Sarah's background is in youth work, social work and youth justice. She is a trained family mediator and has a special interest in positive conflict resolution and restorative justice. Sarah is completing an MPhil with Sheffield University, which is based on research into Family Group Conferencing in Canada.

Jo Pitt is the Development Officer for the Northern half of England for the Parenting Education and Support Forum. She has a special interest in attracting and recruiting parents to courses and in 1999 won a Churchill Fellowship to travel to Australia to look at methods of attracting parents of teenagers used there. From 1992 she ran a pilot parenting project for five years in rural North Yorkshire and is a trained teacher and marriage counsellor.

Helen Richardson is a Research Assistant at the Trust for the Study of Adolescence. A graduate in social policy, Helen is currently working on research projects to do with adolescent health, the parenting of teenagers, and fathering.

Debi Roker is Assistant Director at the Trust for the Study of Adolescence. Debi is responsible for managing the programme of applied research undertaken at the Trust. Her interests are in the areas of adolescent health, youth social activism, strategies to support parents of teenagers, and evaluations of interventions in these areas. She is particularly interested in ways of using research findings, and collaborations between researchers and practitioners.

Dirk Uitterdijk is currently Development Adviser at the YMCA, having previously worked for the Children's Society and a range of charitable and community organisations. Dirk's current role involves supporting YMCA centres that are working with parents of teenagers, and working on a national 'Dads and Lads' parenting initiative.

Subject Index

Name Index

Achenbach, T. 142
Adler, A. 92
Ahmad, W. 44, 45
Ahmed, S. 44
Akister, J. 119
Ali Choudhury, P. 137
Allen, R. 14
Alvarado, R. 93, 99, 102, 104
Alvey, K. 46
Amin, K. 38
Arnold, E. 44
Atkins, J. 195
Attride-Stirling, J. 124

Baginsky, M. 46
Barn, R. 44
Barter, C. 42
Baumrind, D. 28, 67
Behr, H. 161
Bell, R. 8, 15, 16, 203
Berthoud, R. 38, 39, 40–41
Bond, M.H. 68
Borduin, C. 69
Bowen 87
Box, L. 35, 38, 53, 201
Boyd, D. 139–40
Braun, D. 201
Brezina, T. 60
Bright, J. 66
Brook, J. 65
Brooks-Gunn, J. 29, 63, 67
Brown, J. 63
Brown, M. 93
Buchan, L. 126, 137
Bugenthal, D. 31
Burgess, A. 161
Burnard, P. 135
Butler, N. 66
Butt, J. 35, 38, 39, 46, 53

Callan, V. 31
Campbell, S.B. 70
Catalano, R.F. 59
Catan, L. 31
Cernkovich, S. 64
Cherlin, A. 60
Clarke, M. 140
Clemerson, G. 126, 137
Cohen, P. 65
Coleman, J. 8, 10, 14, 19, 25, 26, 28, 31, 33, 35, 39, 40, 43, 45, 63, 81, 86, 100, 163, 179, 198, 200, 204, 205
Collins, A. 31
Collins, W. 65
Cox, A. 137
Crutchfield, R. 64
Cunningham, C. 126
Cusick, J. 86, 200, 201, 205

Daly, B. 141, 142
Davies, H. 83
Davis, H. 124, 125, 126, 135, 136, 137, 140, 141, 142, 182, 200
Davis, P. 137
Day, C. 125, 200
De'Ath, E. 10
Dennison, C. 31
Dickson, D. 135
Dornbusch, S. 67
Dosnajh, J. 45

Eastman, G. 29
Eccles, J. 63
Egan, G. 135
Einzig, H. 7, 17, 18
Elliot, D. 66

Fallowfield, L. 124
Farrington, D. 59, 60, 61–62, 65, 67
Felson, M. 63
Ferdinand, D. 44
Ferri, E. 115
Folkard, K. 15
Forgatch, M. 69